THE STORY OF MAX

Forever in Our Hearts

2008–2020

ROBERT J. CASO

ILLUSTRATIONS BY BILL CASO

Write My Wrongs

Write My Wrongs, LLC, P.O. Box 80781 Lansing, MI 48908
United States
www.writemywrongsediting.com

ISBN: 978-1-956932-11-9

Dedication

This book is dedicated to all animals in need and to the people who rescue them. Please rescue a dog. There are so many who are desperate for a loving home.

Contents

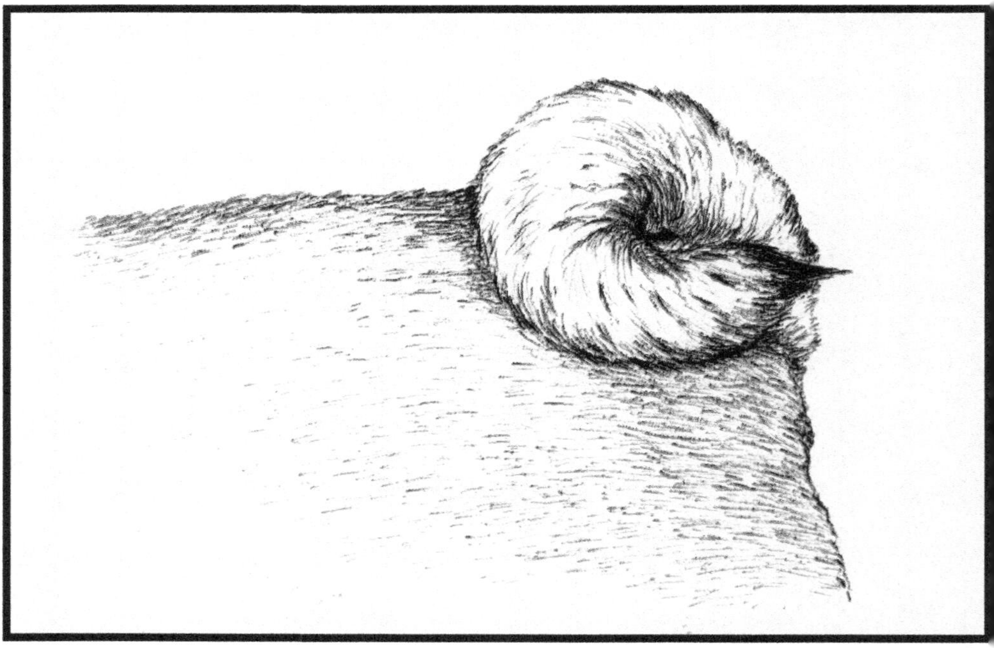

Pug happiness

Introduction

A little boy and his dad were walking along the beach one morning where thousands of starfish had washed ashore after a storm. The little boy started, one by one, throwing the starfish back into the surf. Observing this, his father says to him, "Son, there are so many, how can you possibly make a difference?" The boy thinks for a second, picks up another starfish, and after throwing it into the water, says, "Well, I made a difference for that one."
—Unknown

Let me say first I have never written a book nor have I ever before rescued a dog prior to 2008 when Rikah became part of our family. The impetus behind this effort was twofold. First, I wanted to relive and document my rescue experiences to prevent these memories from slipping further into oblivion. Second, I would like people to get to know our dogs and, in so doing, consider rescuing one of their own so they may have the rewarding experience. Hopefully, another of these amazing creatures might be saved. While it wasn't my original intention to sell this book, I've decided any proceeds will be donated to animal rescue efforts.

In respect to my desire to write a book, I never felt I knew enough about any one subject to write about. Our six rescues, four of which we've had for more than ten years, have since provided me with quite a bit of inspiration. I hadn't thought of doing anything formal until Max passed away. I wanted to write a remembrance of him, but it soon expanded greatly to include the other dogs. The players are six pugs: Rikah, Max, Zoe, Jaxon, Tucker and Lola. The gang was acquired in that order, and five of them are still with us. Collectively, I refer to them as the pug mafia. This book began as a compilation of past emails to my wife of thirty years, Diane, who I would recount the mischief of the day to while she was away on business. Some of it's funny, some of it perhaps not, but it's all true and chronicles my daily life with these creatures.

Interestingly, since I had only rescued cats prior to our dogs, the idea of having a dog never occurred to me. No one in my family had dogs, and of my friends, there was only one who did. While I knew such creatures required a significant amount of attention and care, I was not necessarily against the notion; doing so was simply not something I had seriously entertained. It was Diane's son, Jared, who one day made the recommendation. Diane would constantly steal his rescued pug, Lilly, since the little thing was alone all day while he was at work. Depending on who was available, Diane and I would take turns walking Lilly during the day, and she would be so happy to see us. "Why don't you get your own dog?" Jared finally suggested. So, we did. I got Rikah as a Christmas present for Diane in 2008. The funny thing is it only made the Lilly situation worse since Lilly then had a daily play partner at our place. She'd hide whenever Jared came to pick her up.

Soon after Max died in September 2020, I collected past notes and looked through the many photos I have of him and the others to jog my aging memory. We took Rikah and Max home within about a month of each other, and the first six months with them were so crazy keeping any kind of contemporaneous diary was the last thing I would have thought to do. Nonetheless, my recollections are quite vivid. We took in Zoe and Jaxon as a pair a year later, then it was our two unplanned kids, Tucker and Lola, who unexpectedly showed up maybe eight years after that.

As you might have guessed, Max is the main character throughout. Sometimes, I didn't know whether to laugh or cry as I reminisced about his life with us and agonized over every word in my effort to appropriately portray both him and the effect he had upon our lives. Max may best be described as a cheerful, gentle, and loving soul and a most enthusiastic companion. But what set him apart from our other dogs was his uncanny ability to communicate with humans. Moreover, he had the amazing ability to touch the hearts of everyone he encountered.

Max's introduction to life on earth was most trying for an innocent little puppy, and of our six rescues, his initiation was the worst. During his seemingly brief period with us, Max taught me much about overcoming the challenges life sometimes presents. His eventual and complete transformation to a dog who ultimately would become larger than life itself and be at the center of our six-rescue family amazes me to this day.

At times, it seems as if he has been gone much longer than a year. The world is truly a lesser place without him. Knowing Max, he would never accept seeing sadness in anyone, so he would have never approved of me writing about him while in such a state. There were only two times I ever saw worry in Max's eyes: the day

I met him and the day he died. It was, therefore, with tearful happiness I wrote this, thankful Max chose me to spend his life with.

This is Max's story. I shall miss him for the rest of my days. Perhaps he will think to visit me in my dreams.

Chapter 1
The Story of Max

"...it's a little difficult to know where to start."

While sitting on the couch with our six rescues each night, Diane would oftentimes ask me to recite "The Story of Max" just to see him perk up and smile. He always knew when we were speaking of him, even without mentioning his name. As I told the abbreviated story, with Diane deliberately asking questions about it during the process, Max would look back and forth with interest at whomever was speaking, as if he were actually listening. In reality, he *was* listening. He always loved being the center of attention. My impromptu recitals of his story were necessarily brief, generally focused on the day we met him and how we came to adopt him. Max's story, as you might guess, is much longer than the single event that transpired one cold January evening. So, for me, it's a little difficult to know where to start.

I will, therefore, start at the beginning.

Chapter 2
Go Pay the Lady

"Then, at the height of my apprehension, the most amazing thing happened."

I have often referred to Max as "the dog from heaven," mainly because it was somewhat of an unearthly miracle we wound up with him. Max was the last of a group of puppy mill rescues to find a loving, forever home. In retrospect, the odds against our finding him and his finding us were somewhat astounding. Clearly, a higher authority had meant it to be.

And so, it was.

I began my journey with Max on a cold, late January night in 2009 at a pet store near Parkesburg, Pennsylvania, where the rescue person, Monica of Spanky's Project, had brought him for us to meet. A rather tenuous sequence of events had led to this meeting. During the previous month, Monica had called Diane in desperation after having been inundated by more rescues than she could handle.

What prompted the call was her discovery of a four-page letter Diane had written to the rescuer of our first dog, Rikah. Apparently, no one had ever composed such a comprehensive essay as to why they wanted and deserved a rescue dog. Diane initially declined Monica's offer, explaining a single pet was enough for us to handle. A day or two went by, and Diane happened to relay the story to me, almost as if she were filling me in on current events. To me, it was big news. A bunch of shelter dogs without a home was unacceptable. I asked her to call Monica back and tell her we'd take five, but by that time, Rocky—Max's original name—was the only dog still without a home. So, a meeting was planned.

My inclination to meet Max was not without trepidation. Never having been a dog guy, I was faced with the possibility of having two in rapid succession. And my first wasn't going too well. Throughout my life, I had always found a need to rescue animals, but at this point, the conflict lay in my monthlong experience with Rikah. She was a tiny, tough, and wild little puppy who had been taken away from her mother too soon and tossed around three or four foster homes, likely due to her voracious, sadistic oral tendencies. She made me realize just how much of a rookie I was with her incessant biting, pooping, peeing, running around, and generally not taking no for an answer. At one point in my early relationship with this nutty dog, I walked up the stairs and asked Diane, whose back was toward me, where the dog was. Instead of answering, she turned around, whereupon I saw tiny Rikah hanging by her teeth from Diane's pant leg. Puppy Rikah was certifiably crazy.

The difference between the two dogs upon initially meeting them was shocking. When we met Rikah, she was sitting there packed and ready to go, almost as if to say, "What are we all waiting for?" No kidding. She had a bag beside her filled with her favorite treats and toys. The delay was me finding her even though she was sitting right next to my foot, looking up at me anxiously. She was so tiny the rescue person had to point her out to me, lest I accidentally step on her. It was almost comical.

In contrast, Max was a forlorn little pup. His oversized head was aimed at the floor, and his equally oversized paws had a death grip around Monica's neck. I could see the fright and uncertainty in his eyes as he would briefly look at me and then away, clearly not wanting Monica to release him. He was no doubt petrified by the encounter. It was understandable since Monica, up to that point in Max's life, had been his only shred of security and safety.

I soon learned the poor little guy had been through a lot in his initial two months of life. At the puppy mill, he'd been blinded in one eye from an errant administration of nasal medicine then tossed in a cage with several other similarly mistreated dogs. Max was awaiting euthanasia since he was damaged and could no longer be sold. Heartlessly, the mill had thrown him and all the other dogs in a local dumpster where they were discovered by a man taking out his trash on a cold night in late November. They only had days to live, if that. Their discovery and survival were, frankly, miracles.

Almost like pulling glue off a wall, I extricated Max from Monica's arms and walked him around the pet store. He was shaking when I placed him on the floor, no doubt wondering what I was going to do to him now that he was out from under Monica's protective umbrella. His coat felt like a whisk broom, and it was as white as a ghost. Almost tripping over his gigantic paws, Max wandered through the store with me in tow, occasionally offering a hesitant glance back at me. As we slowly walked, I tried to pet him a few times to help him relax and let him know I wasn't going to hurt him. I would also stop and kneel next to him, telling him it was okay while scratching his ears. Nothing I said or did had much effect. Feeling trapped and helpless, he shook with fear. I felt so horribly bad for him.

As he wandered along aimlessly with his head down, I remember wondering if this was his first time out of a cage or if the poor guy just simply didn't know what to do or where to go. It was almost as if he didn't remember how to walk. The real cold of winter had just begun, and I reasoned he couldn't have been let out to run freely in the open air for long, if at all. And Monica's attention was so diluted Max could receive little individual focus.

I wanted to think the little guy was trying hard to do well on his "interview," but it also seemed he was happy just to be let free for a few minutes in a warm, quiet place and couldn't care less if I liked him or not. I didn't know anything about dogs, but it appeared to me he really needed some down time in a calm, secure, and stable environment.

As I continued to walk Max up and down a few aisles of the store, I gradually concluded he needed not just anyone but us, regardless of whether we knew what we were doing or not. I felt love would conquer all, and I couldn't abandon this downtrodden little guy to the uncertainty of fate by walking away. It was sad for me to see the living result of someone's abuse of an innocent, defenseless, and unsuspecting animal. I thought to myself, *Clearly, these creatures have real, almost human-like feelings. He needs me. How could I possibly say no?* My next thought was a foregone conclusion. *We should take Max home with us.*

Only observing the proceedings to that point, Diane finally made her reservations known. She didn't like Max's disproportionate figure, his unkempt appearance, or his unenthusiastic demeanor. Assuming the role of Captain Obvious, she then pointed out we were busy chasing Rikah around and trying to figure out her, us, and the house, which was a mess. Furthermore, she noted we had yet to master any kind of dog routine, and even with us only having the one, things were getting out of control. Holding my sarcasm in verbal check to avoid an unwinnable battle, I thought to myself, *Thanks for the update, honey.*

The conversation with Diane, as I was walking Max around, went something like this.

"I don't know, Rob, he looks horrible. He smells, he has no personality, and his head and paws are too big for his body. And he has a bad eye."

Max was oddly proportioned, and he looked like a shipwreck survivor. He smelled from the application of something Monica had applied to counter his unfortunate odor, which had exactly the opposite effect, making it worse. We learned Monica hadn't had time to bathe him properly before coming to meet us.

"Yeah, he certainly doesn't look good, honey. But he's been through a lot," I said. "I just feel so sorry for him."

"He can barely walk, and he doesn't really act like a dog," Diane countered. "I don't know. He doesn't even look like a pug."

I happened to glance down at Max at this point in the conversation. He was still standing at my feet with his head and tail down, shaking. His coat was matted and disheveled. And he wouldn't move a muscle. He also didn't resemble anything close to Rikah who was reputedly a purebred pug. And then there was the eye. I realized I was trying to sell the unsalable, but I kept trying.

"Yeah, he doesn't walk like a dog, and I agree with you on the looks. He must have some German shepherd in him or something," I said, grasping at straws. I didn't let her know my German shepherd reference was the only dog breed I could think of in the moment, under wife pressure.

"But you can't be too critical of his looks. After all, he is a rescue, and he hasn't really been cleaned up," I added.

"We already have Rikah, and she's driving us nuts. What are we going to do with another one?"

Captain Obvious had finally gotten me. And with a single rhetorical question. Yes, we were inexperienced, Rikah was still young and seriously crazy, and Monica's call was completely unexpected and untimely. *What are we going to do with another one?* I repeated to myself as I looked away.

We also hadn't yet discussed the possibility of Rikah using Max as a doggie punching bag. I remember being glad she didn't bring that up. It didn't matter, however. Her argument was irrefutably sound as it was. Diane had brought me back to reality. Max was severely traumatized and in marginal physical shape and appearance. Back home, Rikah was well into the process of driving us out of the house. I looked back at my wife, saying nothing. I was taking on water and sinking fast.

It was at that point, I reverted to being undecided and apprehensive, thinking maybe Diane was right, and Max would be better off in another home. I felt like he needed us, but I couldn't help but wonder why he wasn't already taken. He was the last dog of the bunch. Would he ever be adopted? And how does one make such a life-changing decision?

I have always been the type of person who could decide upon a course of action on the spot and under any level of pressure. It was shocking to me I was back on the fence, stifled with indecision. I could feel the tension circling around in my head—logic and reality versus my heart and my inherent need to help this poor dog. Plus, I had the added pressure of my wife to answer to at the end of it all.

I could feel the not-so-good side of my personality starting to surface. When in doubt, procrastinate. Delay. Get more time. Gather more information. Send in the rear guard. *Perfect. That's what I'll do*, I remember thinking.

"Let me give him back to Monica, and we'll talk about it some more," I said. Diane agreed. I bent down, picked Max back up gently, and offered him to Monica.

Then, at the height of my apprehension, the most amazing thing happened.

As I was completing the transfer, Max didn't leap back into Monica's arms. Instead, he settled onto her slowly, glancing back at me with the most intense, affectionate look in his eyes. His gaze went right through me, as if he were telling me he needed us, and he would love us forever if we took him.

Max had just helped my subconscious establish a link between my heart and that miserable logic of mine. At that very moment, I clearly saw Max was a lover, and looking back, I was never wrong about him for a second. With all he had been through, Max could still find love in his heart for humans, the same species who had seriously mistreated him only weeks before. Yes, if Max was a lover, then it was indeed logical I take him home. Decision made.

I stood there for a few seconds looking at him, almost not believing what I had just seen. Before I could question the reality of what I had witnessed, I walked back to Diane.

"I don't know. What do you think?" Diane asked.

Looking hard at her, I said, "Make no mistake. This dog is coming home with us tonight. So, go pay the lady."

For the record, that was the exact exchange; I remember it word for word to this day.

And I loved him already. Max had wormed his way into my heart from which there was no escape.

After completing the transaction, we thanked Monica and walked outside to the car. I tried to shield Max from the biting winter wind. As we drove home, Max in Diane's lap, I resolved to make things right for him, help him, and protect him. I wanted to ensure Max became the happiest dog in the world. I would make it my life's mission.

We were on our way, our great adventure just beginning.

Chapter 3
Bonding with Max

"...our learning experiences were slow, error-prone, hard-won baby steps."

I couldn't help but feel a bit of buyer's remorse over the next week or so after bringing Max home. We now had both an insanely wild puppy and a basket case under the care of two inexperienced owners. It became for us a full-time job of not only trying to figure out what to do but then attempting to do it successfully. Whatever we decided in terms of feeding, walking, outdoor visits, and even nightly accommodations was completely wrong. Almost every day, I would travel to the pet stores, sometimes more than once per day, to procure supplies and various forms of doggie support equipment. Whatever I bought either wouldn't work, didn't fit, or wasn't right. Calls to other dog owners were hit or miss with most of them having grown, well-adjusted pets, not a pair of traumatized puppies. We had to figure it all out on our own. And fast.

Max was rather sick, which further complicated those first few days. He would eat, walk three steps, and poop. His poor health was exacerbated by the unfamiliar surroundings, crazy Rikah, and our uncertain and constantly changing routines. He was also still a very frightened and unsure little dog, undoubtedly from his awful past experience and from all the change thrust upon him.

We tried to maintain some level of normalcy with Max's daily activities, but we had little semblance of such in our own lives at the time, even before we had the dogs. Everything we did in the past, aside from working, was "when we felt like it"—eating, sleeping, going out, doing the wash. Regardless, it became increasingly clear dogs respond well to established patterns and consistency. We also discovered Max was somewhat of a timid eater and would allow Rikah to finish before attempting to dine from their shared plate. This ultimately led to our providing each dog a separate dish, but our learning experiences were slow, error-prone, hard-won baby steps.

At first, we kept Max and Rikah in the kitchen, penned separately in tall, open-topped, plastic fences due to Max's GI issues and our fear bite-happy Rikah would view him as no more than a convenient target. There were dog pee-pee pads everywhere, all over the house wherever the two would go during the day, or where we thought they might go. And, with it being winter, go they did. We had yet to learn their individual warning signs of needing to go out.

But we saw one morning our fears of Rikah wanting to use Max as a chew toy were completely unfounded. And I don't remember a single time Rikah ever bit Max other than playfully. That morning, we were up early, and naturally, went to see how our little rescues were doing penned in the kitchen. Neither of them had heard us approach. Peeking around the corner, we saw Rikah and Max, their paws touching each other's through the plastic lattice of the pen and each of them sleeping up against the common partition. Rikah was beginning to love Max as much as I did, and she was exactly what Max needed. A mother.

It soon became obvious Rikah was way ahead of us when it came to how to take care of and nurture Max. She had a project to keep herself busy, and Max needed all the mothering he could get. *Could this possibly be?* we thought. It was amazing to us that a young, smart-ass little dog—no more than a puppy at the time—could be way ahead of two educated people on how to raise a disabled, frightened, and unsure newcomer. As a result of this observation, the two dogs were never kept in a pen again, and we would find them each morning in the den wrapped up in each other, sleeping. It was a calming sight after the craziness of the first few weeks.

Having Rikah was a godsend to Max and to us. She was the missing link who connected all of us, being almost human herself. She and only she could properly communicate with Max, and he became the son Rikah never had. She would be his mother and co-protector for his entire life.

Rikah as a puppy

Chapter 4
Rikah: Intensity Personified

"And though she be but little, she is fierce."

Rikah is a Dutch female name. We felt it appropriate because pugs were historically a large part of Dutch royalty. Little did we know at the time, assigning a name having such royal overtones to a strong, authoritarian, leader dog would be so perfect.

Rikah is a natural leader, having a level of courage inversely proportional to her size. While this occasionally created competition issues as the group later expanded, to this day, she will automatically lead the way on leash-free walks and rush to high ground to check for adversaries. Utterly fearless, she stands conspicuously atop a knoll and keenly scans in all directions to make sure the coast is clear for her pack. Then she will bark loudly to scare anything away. She's also fond of what I like to call "preemptive barks" as she leaves the house on late night pee-pee outings, presumably to scare the heck out of all the bad guys hiding in the yard. "I'm outside now, so you'd better watch out!" I think that's the message.

Rikah will never be seen last when the entire pack exits the house together; she is on point and in the lead. Always. A considerate and alert leader, she also takes care of her pack. When somebody fails to come in, Rikah will stay outside until everyone is accounted for. At the very least, she will huff while staring me down, which is her way of seeking help to round up the stragglers. Judging from the intensity of her message, it's not a request. It's an order.

I once saw Rikah flush a deer out of the hedgerow that borders one side of our property. I wish I had a video of her barking away and chasing it across the field and down the hill since I don't think anyone believes me. It was one of the funniest "animal things" I've ever seen, but I've frequently wondered what she would have done if she'd actually caught it. I have since referred to her as "Super Dog" and have often thought of getting her a cape with a giant "S" on it, but I can't find one that small.

A quote from Shakespeare's *A Midsummer Night's Dream* fits Rikah perfectly: "And though she be but little, she is fierce." We, however, readily observed our acquisition of needy Max had an immediate and profound effect on Rikah's persona. No longer focusing her attention on the establishment of her dominance over us, Rikah's priority had clearly shifted to overseeing Max and his needs. As she grew and matured that first winter, while also attending to Max more or less constantly, Rikah stopped biting. It was almost as if someone had thrown a switch.

As those early weeks progressed, we continued to see clear examples of her leadership and how Rikah would protect Max, sometimes even from himself. When running through the house, Rikah would oftentimes prevent a still clumsy and careless Max from crashing into chair and table legs by running across his path, diverting him. Remember, Max could only really see from his right eye. How Rikah not only identified but also understood the ramifications of Max's disability is beyond me. It was, however, quite clear she did.

In the ensuing nicer weather, when they could play outside, Max would wander and would absolutely, positively not come back when he was called. He was incredibly incorrigible his entire life, but Rikah would always follow him with a watchful eye wherever he went. Hearing the urgent call, she'd sometimes start a fake fight with him to get him to chase her, with Rikah always running to the source of the recall command, thus bringing Max. *Was Rikah really this smart?* I would often ask myself. But as we grew to know her and see her in action, the answer was unequivocally yes. To this day, she is the mother, the protector, and the leader of her pack. And the boss, of course. And don't you forget it.

Rikah learned very early how to get what she wanted. She has very short hair and seriously dislikes cold weather. Since she was so small, I would sometimes pick her up and stuff her in my jacket to keep her warm. Quickly catching on during our winter walks, Rikah would stubbornly stop in her tracks halfway home and look up at me, waiting for the jacket. She was the boss, and she wanted me to know it.

But whatever you do, don't ever get caught in the intimidating, laser-like Rikah stare, which she does when she wants something. She can turn you into stone with it—just like Medusa. And she always does it to me since I'm the "care, food, and pee-pee guy." I try not to make eye contact when she has me in her sights, but I can't avoid it. Sometimes, I see her doing it, but fake like I don't notice her. She just continues to stare, and when I look back at her, I can see the wheels turning. She is thinking, mixing, planning, evaluating. Rikah will do this every time she has me targeted, and she doesn't blink or look away. It's totally intense, and I don't dare laugh. If it's around dinner time, she will huff, snort, and half bark until I give her my complete and uninterrupted attention. She's in charge of her pack, and her pack is hungry. So, I had better get up and make them all dinner. Or else. Even more amazing is she knows when dinner time is, and she's rarely off by more than ten minutes.

We deduced soon after taking her home Rikah couldn't possibly be all pug, even if her rescuer claimed otherwise. Okay, yes, she looks like a pug for the most part, but her stance, demeanor, elevated intelligence, and Type A persona tell us she has a lot of something else in her. Like English bulldog. Or rottweiler. She's a tough little cookie, which generally isn't a pug trait.

The day we got her spayed and Max neutered, the vet gave us strict instructions they were not to run, play, jump, or do anything that would disturb the stitches. Rikah, being the female, had a giant incision up her belly whereas Max had only a tiny intrusion. You would have thought the opposite was the case the way Max moaned and cried the entire way home. Rikah? No problem. Nary a sound. When we got home, Rikah immediately went into full attack mode, running, jumping, and basically doing everything we were specifically advised against her doing. She wound up splitting her incision, and I, the weak-stomach guy, had to hold it together all the way back to the vet. Thankfully, I was able to defer fainting until later.

Occasionally, Rikah can also be extremely funny. What makes these instances so humorous is they are infrequent and completely out of character. Most bosses don't show a lot of emotion, especially happiness. But mealtime, treat time, and bedtime seem to make Rikah downright ecstatic. It's quite entertaining to see her do the bouncing Rikah hop through the house or down the hallway when she is excited over an announcement we've made. Sometimes, she throws in a pirouette, but it all doesn't last long, lest one of the other dogs see her.

Her play fighting is equally as humorous when another dog, usually Jaxon, starts a mix up. She stares down her opponent, half barks, and makes herself tall on all fours, while hopping back and forth, left and right, thus providing an attacker with an elusive moving target. She is very quick when she does this, making it difficult for an antagonist to get a good shot at her. Rikah is the perfect street fighter.

Max and Rikah developed a strong bond. The two were inseparable. They would eat, sleep, and play together. While Rikah was a master at outsmarting Max by stealing treats or commandeering doggie toys during their horse arounds, Max would ultimately get his way due to his sweet disposition. Rikah would see to that. I frequently slept with them on the couch at night since I stayed up so late. I'd sit and watch television with them, and Max would fall asleep with his head on my lap. He truly loved me, and I loved him back, but it was Rikah who was Max's true savior. Not me.

Some days, I've wondered if Rikah misses Max, or if she's just accepted he's no longer in the pack. It's difficult for me to know or understand how she or any other animal could comprehend such an event and the resulting absence. Perhaps she's just been too busy with the other dogs in the house. If she misses him, she doesn't let it show. Maybe she couldn't. Or wouldn't.

Rikah has been the only remaining link to Max and his life with us. Occasionally, I've thanked her for taking such good care of him. With her being so smart, I think she's understood me. When I've mentioned Max's name, she's looked me straight in the eye, quite intently, and in a noticeably different way than other times I've spoken to her. Like Max, Rikah's an amazingly unique dog but in decidedly different ways. While cerebral, street smart, and tough, she's also a sensitive and loving creature.

In retrospect, she and Max were a perfect combination since each of their personalities complimented the other in so many ways. What a coincidence we acquired two dogs of roughly the same age who needed each other so much.

Sometimes, it's better to be lucky than smart.

Wifey with Lilly on the left, towering Max, Rikah, and the newly arrived twins

Chapter 5
The Rescuers

"Anything worth doing is worth doing to excess."

While I will forever remain an amateur book writer, I do have quite a bit more experience with rescuing all kinds of critters. From cats to snakes that wander into my garage, I try to help them all. Having said that, I still don't like snakes, but they are just trying to survive. Rather than taking them in, I usher them to a more appropriate environment with a long stick.

I like to ride my motorcycles as early as I can in the spring each year, and I oftentimes happen upon box turtles on the side of the road who appear to be waiting for a break in traffic. With their necks stretched to the max, it seems as if they're looking both ways to see who may be coming. I always stop and help them with the realization the three-hour lull they'll need to cross is not going to happen. I sometimes wonder, as I'm carrying one across the road, if where I place them is where the little guy intended to go or if I am just making things worse. But he wanted to get somewhere, after all. We were the ones who interrupted his journey by building a road. At least I got him out of harm's way. That's a good feeling.

Then there are the land-only frogs known as toads. Our dogs, especially Tucker, are inclined to play with them, most likely out of curiosity. It's easy to see how terrified they become, so I discourage the practice by advising the dogs "the frogs are our friends." Okay, they're toads, but you get the idea. And of course, all but Tucker listen to me. The toads almost always wind up in our pool and have no way of getting out. Since they're nocturnal, I dutifully check the pool during our nightly pee-pee missions and scoop them out. Aside from saving them, I'm also avoiding the trauma of a blood-curdling scream from wifey the next morning.

I point to my father as being the source of my inclination to rescue. He loved cats and would always take in the ones who seemed needy or those who didn't have a home. When I was back from college one Halloween weekend, my father and I went to a restaurant that had valet parking. As we were waiting for the car, a friendly black kitten appeared and started purring and rubbing against us. The valet indicated the cat was constantly seen on the restaurant grounds, trolling the dumpster for food. Although she was flea-bitten and skinny, we took her home. My father and I felt an encounter with a black cat on Halloween was pretty spooky. Mom agreed and the name stuck.

Spooky was a most intelligent and endearing companion who wanted nothing more than to sit on your lap and drool while you petted her. She was almost dog-like, and perhaps she was a foreshadowing of things to come in my life. While living with Diane and me, she once ran up the stairs, where she wasn't allowed and never went, and threw a fit to alert Diane the toaster was on fire.

Although Spooky most likely developed some hunting and survival skills when she was alone in the wild foraging for food as a kitten, these skills seemed to have been forgotten or perhaps never matured with age. One beautiful spring day, I spied her in full defilade at the base of the bird feeder pole, looking around, clearly wondering where all the birds had gone.

Spooky, throughout her life, viewed me as her savior, her refuge. I sadly remember the day she came to me, distraught with pain. The vet indicated she had mouth and throat cancer and her survival was doubtful. I had to hand feed her fish, the only thing she could eat without too much pain. I stayed with her night after night and the inevitable day came when I had to say goodbye to her. I cried like a baby when she died and speak of her fondly to this day.

But enough about the rescues. Who are the rescuers? The editors of this book suggested I write something more definitive about us, so you, the reader, would understand what type of people open their home to a sextet of dogs. Contrary to my style and better judgment, I relented. Under protest.

Personality-wise, I categorize myself as a Type A, an ENTP if you subscribe to the Myers-Briggs Type Indicator. It's an abbreviation for Extrovert, Intuitive, Thinking and Perceiving. That designation fits me pretty well, though I am also quite empathetic and always willing to help. This presumes, however, you have at least attempted to help yourself first. I'm a realist, and I pride myself on facts and real-world analysis. My Type B life partner, Diane, continually misinterprets my intentions and often refers to me as a pessimist. This is completely untrue. Pessimists merely think things will go wrong, whereas realists, quite accurately as it turns out, know things will go wrong.

If you haven't already picked this up, I have a rather sarcastic sense of humor, appreciated by only a few. Or perhaps only one. Okay, maybe nobody. The genesis of this unfortunate trait is the result of my growing up in an Italian family headed by an Italian father and only slightly tempered by my German mother. While the latter might seem good to some, she bestowed upon me a large measure of uncompromising perfectionism. So, I am the very embodiment of the worst of all worlds—driven, always right, and stubborn. Everything must be perfect all the time. And even if it is, I still complain. Sarcastically.

I attended Villanova University, initially as an English major with the intention of going to law school. Failing the former, I felt like I'd graduate with no usable skills, so I switched to finance my freshman year, thinking I could still go to law school. I never did go, choosing instead to attend graduate school and get an MBA. During my time there, I flirted with the idea of enlisting in the Navy's Aviation Officer Candidate School (AOCS). I took both the written and physical tests, but I failed the eye test. While I'm lucky enough to say I have few regrets in my life, this is certainly one of them as I'm an avid aviation enthusiast and always have been. I knew in the eighth grade what I wanted to do with my life. I wrote a career paper on attending the U.S. Air Force Academy. While my life undoubtedly would have been quite different, I think the lesson here is not to argue with your dreams. One should simply follow them.

After working for a major public accounting firm, the civilian equivalent of joining the Marines, I worked in the emerging growth biotech and pharmaceutical industries, ultimately becoming controller and later chief financial officer. In retrospect, a fledgling, emerging growth biotech was the perfect arena for a driven, critical-thinking, Type A extrovert. Sure, we had to be experts in the interminable accounting and tax work, but it was never the same day twice.

During those crazy years, I learned being a coach was a lot more valuable than being a boss if I wanted to accomplish anything. I had to garner the best from the people who worked with me since there were so few of us. The company was wildly successful and ultimately acquired by a major pharmaceutical. Proudly, or perhaps sadly, it was only then I realized how good of a team we actually were. Or had. I remember when I announced this monumental event to my battle-hardened staff, just before lunch one day. Their reaction was calm and collected, almost as if they had said, "Okay, Rob, that's great. Now what are we having to eat?" I expected nothing less.

I was later chief financial officer at a few biotechs, each of them betting the house and millions of dollars on a single product. While I didn't mind the environment, I missed the competence and drive of my previous staff. It was shocking to me there were accountants, CPAs mind you, who couldn't reconcile a checkbook much less manage the details of a public offering. These companies either were acquired or had a product rejected by the Food and Drug Administration, sometimes both, so wifey and I started a consulting firm that was surprisingly successful, mostly due to her.

Although accounting and finance could not in any context be considered fun, at least by me, they did facilitate the things I like to do. In fact, I prefer to describe myself by what I like to do instead of what I do professionally. Interestingly, there are a number of crossovers between my professional and personal life. Some even apply to my dogs.

Working was something I did when I wasn't playing with my scale model airplanes, motorcycles, and cars. While these are sometimes referred to as toys, I resent the designation and prefer instead to view them as art forms. Which they are. I designed and flew my first model at age eight, so it was pretty clear where my passions lay. These days, I start with a blank CAD (computer-aided design) screen and wind up with something that flies. Many of my models have been in magazines and contests. The crossover with my professional life is the drive needed to reach the end of the project and focus on all the required steps along the way. It is, however, a most unforgiving hobby in that the slightest of errors or oversights will be dealt with severely in the form of a catastrophic crash. But this is true with rescuing as well. The reward for success is commensurate with its risk—as it should be.

I liken my motorcycles to my rescued dogs in that they wouldn't be what they are today if it weren't for me. A few wouldn't be on this earth. Some came from bad homes or were about to be tossed away and forgotten. Others arrived with damaged or missing parts, and most had evidence of ill treatment. They needed me to set things right. To work on them. To love them. Just as with dogs, some people should not own a motorcycle. They treat the machines with no more reverence than an everyday toaster.

Just like my years in finance, I have seen it all with motorcycles. When taking them apart, what I find is never surprising, but it's always amazing. I have newer bikes that were bought from the motorcycle pet store, and they spoil me with their competence and reliability. But most do not have the charm or character of one that has been saved. Rescued bikes are much like rescued dogs. We have a special relationship. I've been riding since age seventeen, and I used to race vintage bikes. I've also had the life experience of riding in the Alps, which was downright terrifying at times. The unfortunate reality is my dogs, over the past ten years or so, have been somewhat constraining in terms of me being able to go anywhere far away. I love our dogs, so such is life. But I still have my bikes.

Last are my cars. Since the air-cooled Porsche 911 is my favorite car in the history of the civilized world, I challenged myself by taking in a couple of old 911s. Like my dogs and motorcycles, these cars needed me. But I was well-prepared. My high school friend Rudy and I would steal his dad's mostly red Porsche 356 coupe and go for joyrides in our never-ending quest to meet girls. While this may sound like great seventeen-year-old fun, his car required us to get it running and had nary a straight piece of sheet metal anywhere. And no heat. I'm sure Rudy's dad was aware of what we were doing, but he presumably let us do what we wanted since it was cheaper than bailing us out of jail or paying for drug therapy. Plus, we got his car running. His thinking also could have been we were learning a valuable skill and becoming problem solvers by trying to get a spark across a set of badly worn ignition points. Now a bit wiser and perhaps jaded, I think he deliberately sabotaged the car immediately prior to each of our attempted felonies just to keep us busy. Much to our dismay, Rudy and I eventually came to the sad realization we were a lot better at getting that thing to run than we ever were at meeting girls.

My wife Diane is a total Type B introvert. She knows any frontal assaults will be readily repelled by me and done so with alarming rapidity. But with her, it's all surprisingly effective flanking maneuvers, even when I know they're coming. My wife is the type of person who if she told you to go away, you'd actually look forward to taking the trip. As such, and in stark contrast to me, everyone she encounters loves her, including the dogs. I guess the average between us is about right, and our relationship is the truest illustration of opposites attracting.

The one thing we do have in common is the belief "anything worth doing is worth doing to excess," as evidenced by our having six dogs at one point. Another example is the four-page treatise she wrote to the foster people, explaining why we were the best home for Rikah, our first rescue. Rikah was a collaborative Christmas present, and Diane's dissertation was instrumental in our acquiring her. Had Diane not penned the letter, we would never have gotten to Max. The world works in wonderfully strange ways sometimes.

Diane did have a dog, Joey, in high school, but I describe us both as newbies because when it came to rescuing, we were horribly inexperienced with the issues these creatures bring with them. She knew and understood a bit more than I did about a dog's personality, but it was still a game of trial and error for both of us.

Professionally, Diane also worked in the pharmaceutical industry but on the sales and marketing side. At one point, we both worked for the same company. We were already married by then, and it was during that period we saw each other the least. Her expertise resides in developing these convoluted sales and leadership training programs that use words I never thought went well together in the same sentence. But everybody loves them. When we acquired our six unruly rescued dogs, I thought, *Perfect. I'll just have her write up one of those fancy training programs so order and discipline might be restored.* She never did, but I doubt if one would have worked anyway. I like the training program for finance a lot more because it's simple, fast, and easy to understand: "Figure this out, and let me know when you have it." You never have to work on any one thing for very long either since there's always a deadline. Like tomorrow.

Diane's primary hobby is kids, kids, and more kids, including her own from a prior marriage, Jared and Stephanie, and the grandkids. In fact, kids are her only hobby. The definition of the word "hobby" is a constant struggle between us since I consider mine the only real ones. Of course, our amusements collide when I let the kids sit on my bikes and then teach them how to clean up fingerprinted gas tanks. Birthday parties get a bit crazy at times with all the kids, noise, and rescued dogs running around, sometimes in costumes. Motherly Rikah loves kids, so she's in her element during these events.

Although she had always wanted to attend college, Diane had no such degree when we met, so I pushed her to get one. This was a big mistake as she would later become a professional student. She eventually graduated with multiple academic awards, some of which I had never even heard of. It was a truly humbling experience for me since the pinnacle of my college career was the attainment of a "B," whereas to her, such a lofty height was viewed as being at the bottom of the barrel. All a matter of perspective, I guess.

Since wifey is one of those touchy-feely marketing people, she prides herself on her ability to read the body language and facial expressions of our dogs. Max, in particular, was an almost human-like communicator in this regard and adept at manipulating Diane to get exactly what he wanted at the moment. Through her, he worked his evil magic on me, and the result was Max was able to keep both of us as his lifelong, personal servants. But all our dogs communicate with us in some fashion, sometimes quite humorously, so the game is to know what to look for. Diane detects these subtleties instantly. While I have gotten better at it over the years, I still have somewhat of a tin eye when it comes to reading them, so I rely on her to tell me what's really going on. And true to form, the dogs would much rather congregate around Diane on the couch than they would with me. They also run to her with overwhelming enthusiasm when she enters the room. In their eyes, Diane is the fun social director, the mommy, and the cuddler, and I am the boss, the protector, and the leader of the pack.

Chapter 6
Barking vs. Growling

"...the cat is our friend..."

I had rescued cats for just about my entire life. My last cat, an elderly female named Porsche, was still with us when we got the dogs. Falling prey to the false narrative cats and dogs don't mix, I kept them separated as much as possible. But Porsche was set in her ways and throughout her life, only liked me. She would sit on my lap and would not care for or acknowledge attention from anyone else. I surmised a pair of active, crazy puppies would not mix well with a singularly focused feline, and their mere presence might ultimately devolve into a territorial dispute.

I spend protracted periods of time working in the basement on various, or in Diane's mind meaningless, projects. The dogs congregating around her on the couch would get anxious since the entire group wasn't together. Since they had frequently witnessed Diane summon me via her cellphone, and upon her doing so, I always magically appeared, they began pawing that magic black box themselves to get me to show up. It worked.

The basement was also where Porsche lived, and she would sleep atop my worktable in a kitty bed. Rikah visited me one day in the basement, and quickly spying the cat, she began barking. I carefully explained to her the cat is our friend and barking at the cat is, therefore, prohibited. To support my position, I cited the provisions of the well-established house "no barking" statute. Rikah looked at me very intensely while I explained this to her and to my amazement, summarily stopped barking. She appeared to understand. Perfect. I felt we had reached a new plateau in our relationship.

After looking at me for a few seconds, Rikah focused back on the cat. She then, after a minute or two more, resorted to growling. I'm sure when the statute was written, the lawmakers felt any reasonable man would conclude growling was a form of barking, and it would also be similarly prohibited. However, the word "growling" was not specifically mentioned.

Could it be our Pug was trying to outsmart me by exploiting a loophole in the "no barking" rule? Or did she sincerely think it was okay to growl?

Perhaps this was an issue for a higher court to decide.

Inquisitive Max

Chapter 7
Teaching Max

"...I had to teach him how to negotiate steps."

The normalcy in his life helped Max overcome his abuse, and we could see him gradually come out of his shell. It was clear as the days progressed my initial assessment of him was correct. Max was a most gentle and loving creature. His tail was up and in a constant curl, and he would no longer walk with his head down. There was an enthusiastic bounce in his step and a revealing wag in his tail. He'd greet Diane and me in the morning with a giant, tonguey smile, and you could see the excitement in everything he did. It was at this point I learned dogs can smile and exhibit telltale facial expressions, and Max, for his entire life, would talk with his ears and eyes. Max was beginning to love life, and I was thrilled for him. He was becoming king.

While quietly lounging on the couch with us in the evening, Max would hang onto our every word, listening for his name, or any other phrase he recognized, to be mentioned. If we said his name, his ears would spring up, he'd raise his head, and then he'd look eagerly at the person who spoke. If a conversation ensued, he'd turn and look at every player, and if you began to laugh, Max would try to laugh too. One night, while we were watching television, I leaned toward Diane and referred to Max as "the big dog." You would have thought I had called him for dinner! Max jumped right up and started panting.

As Maxie settled in, and after multiple trips to the vet, his health improved. That allowed Diane and me time to focus on exactly how we were going to raise these two and what the goals were.

During his initial two months or so, I had to teach him how to negotiate steps. He was terrified of steps, either going up or down, and they remained a formidable obstacle to Max his entire life. I realize he was hampered by a bad eye and the depth perception issues that went along with it, but he was simply afraid of them regardless. I guess I can understand. To a small dog, going up must look like scaling a mountain and going down a cliff. But Max really wasn't a small dog per se, and Rikah got the whole thing immediately, zipping up the stairs on her first try even though the step risers were about twice as tall as she was. She'd go vertical—couch, steps, chairs, whatever—anytime she was playing with Max and wanted to outmaneuver him. Such as after stealing one of his treats.

While Max remained timid and unsure, I was adamant he be taught how to climb the stairs. Figuring descending a flight of steps was a lot scarier than ascending, I would situate him at the bottom and encourage him to go up. It was like trying to train a toddler. Keeping the risk of failure and the potential for injury in check, I would place one of Max's giant paws on the first stair, only to have him pull it away.

"Come on, Max. You can do it!"

We'd do that for what seemed like fifteen minutes, Max preferring to remain exactly where he was. But at least he was smiling! To Max, all I was doing was teaching him a new game. His excitement level would drop, however, when I picked him up and placed both of his front paws on the first step. He wouldn't budge. Next, I'd pick up his back half while moving his foremost paws forward. Still nothing. I had to repeat the sequence all the way to the top. Front. Back. Front. Eventually, we made it, laughing as we reached the summit. Then I'd pick Max up, bring him back downstairs, and start the process all over again.

"Come on, bud. Let's try this again!"

In time, Max got it. Kinda. If he had a clear objective and wasn't thinking about it, he could fly right up the stairs. But other times, he'd stop halfway, paralyzed with indecision, and look to me for help. Or he would traverse most of the steps then stop cold when he was three or four from the top. If there was another dog or group of dogs in his way, forget it. He wouldn't move an inch until I cleared the way.

The same could be said for the couch where all the dogs liked to lounge. Max had to be in his spot, and he didn't like it when the other dogs were in it. When I would move to help him up, he'd then jump with no assistance. It was maddening. Another game, perhaps? All in a day's work for Maxie. Once he was on the couch, he would grin at me and settle in. I could never tell whether he was happy about his achievement or just laughing at outsmarting me. On second thought, it was probably about the attention. Max had to be the center of attention. Always.

Our ongoing objectives were relatively easy to see—treats, playing, excessive feeding, teasing, chasing, walking, roughhousing, and sleeping with them each night at the end of the day. Above all, Diane and I tried to give the two dogs a set routine and a consistent feeding, walking, socializing, and sleeping schedule. We would repeat the routine each day as best we could, and it was one of the few things we did right. With little aberration in the process during those cold winter months, the two became accustomed to the normalcy, the secure environment, and our constant attention. And to a never-ending stream of treats and toys.

After a few months with him healthy and growing, and with the weather improving, it soon became obvious what Max was all about: he just wanted to have fun.

Chapter 8
The Spring of All Springs

"...our two pugs had prevailed."

When Max was about six months old, spring arrived. Gone was the cold and the biting wind of winter. And it had seemed like such a long one. Warm breezes were beginning to mix with faint remnants of the cool, and things were growing, including our two rescues. There was life all around us, an appropriate metaphor for our two pugs. They were alive, happy, and free. For me, it was a spring like no other since Max was now healthy, active, and beginning to explore his new world under Rikah's protective eye. I hadn't realized at this point in each of their young lives, neither had experienced warm weather. It was a new and exciting world for them, especially for Max, and it was an interesting perspective for me to ponder while watching the two explore and play. Max had finally found his nirvana in the warm outside world of springtime.

It was thrilling for Diane and me to see them love their lives and how they'd grown to love each other. Despite all the confusion and change over the previous months, combined with our disorganization and lack of experience, our two pugs had prevailed and were now thriving. I couldn't help but feel proud of them both. And it seemed to me all we did was provide a place for them that didn't have snow in it.

Max's newfound confidence was, however, the proverbial double-edged sword. Restless, rambunctious, and now a healthy guy filled with coursing, young male hormones, all Max wanted to do was explore, run, and play. We'd let them run free in our spacious, fenced-in yard, but the confined plot wasn't as much fun as the wide-open world. I knew it, and they knew it too. They sought to conquer the unknown universe on the other side of the fence, and they wanted to do it by themselves.

I sympathized with this point of view, which is why I would let them occasionally roam beyond the confines of our yard without the pressure of two nagging parents. *What's the point of having a life if there's no fun in it?* I thought. Let's face it, parents aren't much fun, and given my excessive focus on the two, I had become mine.

Of course, Max couldn't realize the limits of our secure environment or those of Rikah's protective umbrella. When let outside on a nice day, he'd zoom off to parts unknown with little Rikah furiously trying to keep up with him. While it was amusing to observe these proceedings the first few times, I soon realized this was a recipe for trouble with two worrisome parents calling them back to no avail. On more than one occasion, I had to chase them down with my ATV to search for them. I knew if I found one, the other couldn't be far away, and that was most often the case.

Although Pennsylvania is not normally known for having a significant variety or population of voracious creatures, particularly in inhabited areas, running into only one would probably have been enough for Max. Inexperienced and unaware, he would have been easy pickings, and I'd constantly worry about this when he would escape and wander. Diane and I would sometimes be more concerned about Rikah. Although she'd most likely be a fierce opponent, we surmised her size would take her only so far in a serious engagement.

The complicating factor was Rikah was still a puppy too, and although extremely smart and alert, she often succumbed to the inclination to discover her new world. One time, I found them both about a half mile away on an adjoining farm, just about to shuffle off into the woods. It was a new distance record for the two. They saw me approaching, and Max immediately shifted into "let's play" mode, preferring to run away just as I got within arm's reach. While I understood he could not possibly grasp the gravity of the situation, it was the final straw for me. The wandering had to stop.

On other occasions, the two would randomly visit some of the neighbors. The apparent criteria for those visits was whoever happened to be outside. And in the spring, that was just about everybody. Being both the new kids on the block and genuinely friendly, the duo soon became neighborhood celebrities. The neighbors were nice enough to shepherd them over to me when they saw me come looking. Still, the running away was a problem. After about two weeks of searching for them, we resorted to leashing them each time they went out where there wasn't a doggie fence.

Parents are so un-fun.

Chapter 9
The Harness

"...she was equally skillful at getting out."

Even something as simple as using a leash was entirely new to me. While I certainly knew what they were, with pugs, you cannot simply throw one around their necks and call it a day. Pugs have sensitive breathing apparatuses and, therefore, nothing can go around their necks. I was advised early on that, no, I had to get a special leash. A harness. These things go around their front legs and snap together over their shoulders. Harnessing, as you might have guessed, was also new to our two dogs, and the process of getting them on a pair of squirming, excited puppies added an additional dimension to the going out or walking routines each day. Sometimes two or three times a day.

While smartie Rikah got the process down pat probably the second time we did it—almost to the point where she would walk into the thing—that was never the case with Max. Getting him into the harness was almost as much exercise for me as the walk itself. Harnessing up in Max's eyes was simply another game for him to play. This wasn't helped by my first telling him we were going out, which would initiate his trademarked circling in place at high speed. Eventually, it didn't matter whether I told him or not. The mere act of me getting the harnesses ready for the pair was clue enough. Instant craziness.

Finally getting him to settle down, I would kneel and place the harness on the floor, just at his front paws. Max would then circle away a few feet, just out of reach. It was so hard to get mad at him since he was smiling with his tongue out the whole time. I would move closer and repeat the process and then so would he. He'd consume a surprising amount of real estate playing this game, requiring me to knee-walk through almost the entire house.

This continued until I got smart one day and started the process with his back to a door or some other obstacle. I'd lay the contraption in front of him as I had done before. Next, I would take both of his paws, position them in the harness, and pull it up over him in one move. He still made me chase him around the house on occasion when he would outsmart me. Just for fun.

Although Rikah was by now a pro at getting into her harness, she was equally skillful at getting out. She was so small that if I didn't have the thing adjusted perfectly, she could shrug it off at will. With them growing almost daily when they were puppies, I had to make changes to their harnesses every week. Or buy new ones. Inevitably, I would get it wrong by fractions of an inch, which was a rather large error factor on Rikah.

She also would rid herself of the restraint for no apparent reason at all, probably to reaffirm to me her status as boss. As she settled down over the years, today remaining in her harness during our walks for the most part, I think what she's attempting is some kind of smart-ass doggie cold war. She remains in her harness merely to appease me since I am the ultimate leader of our pack.

But she knows, and she knows I know she knows, she can escape at will.

"Wasn't me, didn't do it!"

Chapter 10
Bad Max

"...heads I win, tails you lose."

Max was never really bad as a puppy, but he was mischievous. When he would disappear in the house for more than a few minutes, we surmised Maxie had found something of greater interest than sitting around watching TV, being fed a constant stream of treats. We always hoped it was a dog toy he had rediscovered, but it usually wasn't. One time, I carelessly left an entire roll of paper towels within easy dog reach. What a mess. But what fun! Open doors to bathrooms were another invitation for Max with similar result. Diane and I would yell, "No, Max!" so often when he was a puppy when it came time for us to determine a name for our consulting firm a few years later, we considered naming it "Nomax and Associates."

Most of Max's naughtiness as a puppy centered around his constant yearning to go out and explore. Once he managed to get outside untethered, it was a real job getting him to come back. Max made his exploration intentions very clear if I interrupted him while he was running away. He would stop in his tracks, turn to look at me, and then evaluate my request. I could see him thinking. He would look in the direction he really wanted to go and then back at me to see exactly what I was going to do and if I was serious. It was a losing battle. If I went after him, he would run away in the direction he wanted to go, and if I retreated, he'd simply ignore me. A "heads I win, tails you lose" situation. It was at that point I learned if you chase a dog, he will run away. If you run from a dog, he will likely chase you, but that wasn't always the case with Max.

The amazing thing was that Max, for all his naughtiness, never displayed a hint of remorse. I could yell at him, tell him he was a bad dog, or put him in solitary in the den, otherwise known as Max's room. At the end of it all, he'd think it was just one big game and couldn't wait to do it all over again. He'd be smiling and wagging during one of my half-hearted dress downs, with me struggling to refrain from laughing myself. Then Diane would yell at the both of us. While solitary sounds bad, keep in mind that the solitary room in the rescue house was replete with fresh doggie water, blankets, pillows, dedicated doggie beds, and play toys. Sometimes, there were unpoliced treats laying around, which Max would find immediately. So, to him, the end result of being bad was something a lot closer to fun than it was to punishment.

To make things worse, Rikah would throw a fit if Max wasn't with the rest of the family. She would have none of that since Max was Rikah's only child, and in any case, she didn't issue the discipline order. Rikah would stand in front of the windowed door of the den and observing Max's predicament, turn to me with a hop, a stern look, and perhaps some half barks. Max would be looking at me with his tongue out as if to say, "See? I told you! You'd better let me out before Rikah gets mad!"

And so, we would. He'd emerge wagging his tail, looking for the next thing to get into. Or proceed to jump up on the couch with the other dogs, later including Zoe and Jaxon, who would give him a royal welcome. Collective tail wags, smiles, kisses, and an uptick in group excitement would ensue. They were no help at all. Then we would give them all treats, otherwise known in the rescue house as "team treats." These were rewards given for absolutely no reason whatsoever. Bleeding-heart Diane instituted that one. I had nothing to do with it.

Max, through Rikah, was becoming the boss. He knew Rikah would always rush to his defense and relied on her to reduce his detention periods. He would use this against us time and time again. He was that smart.

Between Rikah and us, we created a diva in Max. Of course, this only made me love him more.

Chapter 11
A Walk in the Park

"Women in jogging shorts were at particular risk of being maimed..."

Full-bred pug siblings Zoe and Jaxon ("the twins") joined our pack of two about a year after we brought Max home. I'd frequently take the four of them to the local park for what I thought would be a pleasant, relaxing doggie stroll on a sunny day. Maybe all of us would cuddle together on a park bench, enjoying nature and listening to the birds. That was the idea, anyway. Ha!

Although they sound inviting, such trips were not for the faint of heart. As if the leashing up, getting them into the car, getting them there, and getting them out wasn't enough, I first had to chase them around the house and make sure I had all the required doggie support equipment like plastic bags, two water bottles, and towels for the muddy-paw ride home. I often toyed with the idea of bringing along a Rambo knife just in case the dogs tied me up in the leashes to the point where escape was impossible, but I decided to risk it. I just never left home without the basics.

The real insanity began when we entered the park, shattering my vision of a peaceful outing. While they could only see the tops of the trees upon driving in, the numerous speed bumps along the entrance were a dead giveaway. Zoe would be sitting on my lap looking out the driver's window, and Rikah would be running back and forth, attempting to knock Zoe off. Sometimes a fight would break out on my lap. Jaxon would be milling around, and Max would start barking and making his way to the door. Or more accurately, Max would be howling. On Max's cue, the rest would join in. The craziness then ticked up as I parked and shut the engine off. Or maybe they sounded louder without the competing noise. Either way, I had to fight for the exit while pinned against the driver's door with the five of us attempting to get out all at once. Alive.

The simple act of opening the door became a major feat and invited an even greater frenzy. And the slightest bit of carelessness by me facilitated an escape, with the escapee running through the park's tranquil aura at full speed, trailing the leash. I later got smart and gathered the leashes as I attempted to exit. Eventually, I somehow got them all down to the ground safely, although the exact process varied each time. A combination of guiding them, catching them, and blocking them as each attempted to leap or fall from the car, sometimes all together. It was as if the car was on fire. Apparently, nobody wanted to be the last one in the park. Especially Rikah. She always had to be first.

The ensuing walk in the park would be anything but. After untangling myself and getting everybody pointed in more or less the right direction, "into the wind" as I used to call it, another dog would either be visually targeted or heard. It was almost like clockwork since the park is a popular place for dogs. Even someone walking on the asphalt trail was enough to set them off. This provoked yet another round of excitement, with the entire sled team screaming and pulling on the leashes with all their collective might and with the motivation of an unfed pit bull.

Observers of this madness recommended I take them to see a doggie trainer. Yeah, right. One look at this mob and a dog trainer having any kind of sense would run away or risk being transformed into a mumbling, drooling fool. In fact, the only dog trainer I'd ever consider taking them to would be the one having enough sense not to even entertain the idea. Doggie trainer, huh? Right. Forget it.

Delaying the walk were the other people at the park. Sure, they were nice enough, but just about all of them who happened to notice my group had to then meet the snarling grumble of pugs. I used to tell people as they approached the pack was vicious or hadn't been fed, but such warnings had little effect as a deterrent. Onward they came. Women in jogging shorts were at particular risk of being maimed as the unruly quartet jumped, clawed, and howled as if to say, "Pet me! Pet me!" I'd repeatedly say, "Don't jump!" to no avail. Max, of course, was in his social element, but it was always Rikah who garnered the most attention due to her size.

"That's Rikah. She's the boss," I would inform people, but nobody believed me because she was so small. "How do you tell them apart?" and "Are they all brothers and sisters?" were the most common questions I got. In the beginning, I would go into my usually boring, long-winded explanation. But it soon became apparent I would never accomplish my mission of completing a single lap around the park with these maniacs if I continued to provide informative answers. In the interest of expediency, I henceforth deferred to the less than honest "I can't" and "I don't really know."

Once the group was settled, we could begin the endless monotony of the circuitous walk around the park. Twenty feet later, however, somebody would have to take an excitement poop or needed a drink of water. So, we'd all have to stop. I then had to fumble with the water bottles and plastic bags while holding onto four straining leashes. They would then fight for water like they'd been in the Sahara for days.

Rikah, Zoe, and Jaxon could drink from a standard water bottle without wasting too much, but as you can imagine, Max was a mess. Usually, he didn't even want a drink, but succumbing to the peer pressure, he would take one because everybody else did. Max would only drink if I supplied him a dangling dribble from the bottle. The result was most of it never got to where it needed to go. Hence the two bottles. The dribble also had to be the correct velocity and volume. Too slow and he would lose interest, too fast and he would shake his head and walk away. It had to be just right.

About halfway around, my troupe would settle into their prescribed formation and begin to walk ahead of me in their familiar rhythm and purpose. I always enjoyed the sound of sixteen paws clicking away on the asphalt as the group excitedly rambled toward the objective. Little did they know the objective was to get back to the car in one piece and with everyone still in tow. Further distractions would mostly be ignored along the way, but I still had to maintain our distance from other dogs. Rikah, of course, would bark at the enemy birds and squirrels. The twins were happy walking together in their comfortable cadence. And Max, well, he'd just trot along with his tongue hanging out per usual. He loved the pack, the park, and our walks. I loved them all too, despite the craziness.

Chapter 12

A Dumpster Dog with a Gourmet Palette

"...it couldn't possibly be that complicated to get two dogs to eat."

During his young life, I could see where things were going with Max since he demanded so much focus from us and Rikah. A brief internet search provided the perfect description. Prima Donna: "a diva who insists on special treatment." In other words, a spoiled brat, which was just about as accurate as it got in Maxie's case. I had only myself to blame since I regularly festooned him with constant and instant attention. As a result, I became Max's servant. Shamelessly, I loved every minute of it.

As Max's health improved, he began to eat. And eat. And eat. But this was only after we solved the food issue. Diane and I would try different dog foods, attempting to find the ones that were best for him and Rikah as they grew and got bigger. It was all happening so fast. I would stand in the supermarket or pet store aisles reading dog food cans for what seemed like hours. The same person would walk by me three or four times, and I would still be there reading cans. Even with my glasses, the packages were impossible to decipher since the print was so small, and I'd never heard of half of the ingredients. How was I supposed to determine what was good or bad for them?

I would wind up buying an entire case of what I thought was the best food, and then they wouldn't eat it. Back to the store. More standing and reading. Then I would buy another brand and get the same result. Not wanting to take another financial risk, I'd buy a can or two of a third brand. They would eat that, of course, and I'd have to run back the next day to buy more. But the store would be out of it. Or a clerk would tell me it was discontinued. How can you discontinue chicken? Or fish? I'd stand and read some more, seeking and ultimately selecting a fourth brand that appeared to have the same ingredients as the food they liked. Thinking I had it all figured out, I'd confidently buy a whole case of the new stuff, but then they wouldn't eat it. Or they'd just pick at it. It was maddening.

To further complicate things, one dog would eat what I bought, and one wouldn't. Sometimes, they would eat something one day and ignore it the next. It was difficult for me to ascertain whether that reaction was just a temporary one or if they didn't like it permanently. We had so many half and unopened cans of dog food lying around we could've opened our own store. Thinking I'd be able to trick the two of them, I tried mixing the good stuff with remnants of the bad stuff so we could at least use some of it up. With the good stuff now contaminated, they wouldn't eat it.

I tried to understand the secret formula. I'd open a can, take a whiff, and attempt to differentiate the key ingredients that made one kind acceptable and the other not. But it all looked and smelled the same to me. And the consistently inconsistent results told me it all probably was.

As I so often did when faced with an insurmountable problem, I stepped back and evaluated the objective and the means by which I could achieve it. I had to get Max and Rikah to eat (the objective), and I had food on hand and within easy reach (the means). I ate all the time, so it couldn't possibly be that complicated to get two dogs to eat (connecting the means to the objective). After all, we all got hungry. The vet had told us to serve Max rice every so often to calm his GI issues, which we did, so cooking was already an option. It seemed like the obvious answer, but when I asked around, not many dog owners cooked for their dogs. It just wasn't the prevailing pet protocol. But I was running out of options. *To hell with this*, I thought.

I thought back to the motorcycle trips I would take to see my longtime friend, Greg, in Lake Placid, New York. He had rescued mastiffs over the years, a number of whom I had met before I had my crazies. Those dogs were so big you could almost ride them, and he would feed them just about anything. I witnessed him more than once throwing a Big Mac in the general vicinity of his dog, who not only caught it on the fly but swallowed it in one gulp without even chewing it. *Oh, okay,* I thought. *I get it. Dogs will eat anything you provide.* That's what I concluded after observing the proceedings. But with their picky, gourmet eating habits, my pugs erased another one of my preconceived notions.

Under ever-increasing dog pressure, I tried cooking for them. I knew what was going into every meal, and I was determined to make it something I would eat myself—if only in a pinch. Naturally, they liked what I made, so I became a full-time chef for two snotty, gourmet dogs. And later, I cooked for the entire pack. I was the food guy, and the dogs would come thundering over whenever I was in the kitchen. It didn't matter what I was in there for at the time.

"Hey, everybody! The food guy is in the kitchen," I imagined them saying. "Let's see what's going on. Maybe we can get some."

Diane and I taught the four dogs to sit if they wanted a treat or an ad hoc, unscheduled offering from the table or refrigerator. It was difficult for me to turn down a row of begging pugs, looking up at me with pleading eyes. Zoe and Jaxon have the routine down to a science. They sit perfectly and patiently as they await their offering, which is why they are the fattest. Rikah almost never sits, but sometimes she rewards me with a fake sit, a move resembling a curtsy. I let her get away with it because rank sometimes has its privileges. Max would sit with his hind legs splayed, and he'd drool and make anxious whining noises if I happened to get to him last. "Okay, Okay, Max. It's coming," I would say, but this only made him want the treat more.

After finally solving the food issue, Max wanted to eat twenty-four hours a day, seven days a week. I remember oftentimes feeding him in the middle of the night. But he wasn't getting fat, he was getting big. It was thrilling for me to see him getting larger, healthier, and more active, with the rest of him finally catching up to his giant head and paws. To this day, I tell people I'm like an Italian mother—one who equates food with love.

Max liked to lick the plate clean. His entire life, if I took his dish away from him before he had a chance to polish it with his tongue, he would look up at me and sulk. He was also afraid of the noise the plastic plate made when it moved, so I'd go through great pains to keep it still. This meant I had to monitor how close he was to finishing his meal and then, at the precise moment, walk in the room and hold the plate for him so he could lick it without it making any noise. Max would only lap up the leftovers if I held it steady for him. Twice a day, 365 days a year, it was hysterical watching him attempt to tease that last little bit out from under the edge of the plate. With his long tongue, he'd be ultra-careful not to move it, but in doing so, he'd create a screeching plate sound. In retrospect, I should have provided him with a different plate. A fancy one. Perhaps a giant doggie bowl with a rubber bottom with his name on it. Being such a diva, Max would have loved a special dish, and the other dogs would have taken notice.

Max wouldn't eat with the other dogs in the kitchen, so we gave him his own room in which to dine. The den. We referred to it as Max's room, which I alluded to before. During one of our check-in calls with Monica, she noted Max's timidity with food was likely the result of him having to share meals with twenty or so other dogs subsequent to his rescue. The older dogs would crowd him, so he wouldn't eat until everyone else was finished. With us, Max was very particular about not only having his own space but the proper location of the plate in the room when you served it to him. If it wasn't in the right spot, he wouldn't eat. Due to all these special accommodations, we started referring to what Max did as fine dining. After all, the den was a really nice room.

Not only was he a timid eater, but he was a very slow, tentative, and rather annoying eater. If I ever wanted to get information out of anyone against their will I would simply force them to watch Max eat. It would generally take him twice as long as the other dogs to finish a meal, and if I didn't provide him with a separate dining room, the other dogs would snipe his food. But it was really Max's own fault his meals took him so long to finish. First, he'd take a sniff to see if it was something he liked. If he didn't, he'd back off and shake his head then sit next to his plate and look at me. Occasionally, that would mean he wanted me to hand-feed him. Yes hand-feed him. Can you believe it? If the meal had potential, then Max would move to the opposite side of the plate and take another whiff. He might even perform a lick test. The test would make a quarter of the food fly off the plate, so Max would walk back to where he started and sniff what was covering the floor. When he should've been eating, he was literally traversing his meal.

Since the vet advised us to feed Max rice, we occasionally and regrettably did When Max attempted to eat a meal containing the starch, however, it wound up looking like a car bomb exploded in the room. There was rice everywhere. I referred to it as the "Max blast radius." It would then take him a half hour just to clean up the mess. But he was so fastidious, he didn't miss a morsel. Despite how long it took him, I was just thrilled he was eating at all—I mean, dining.

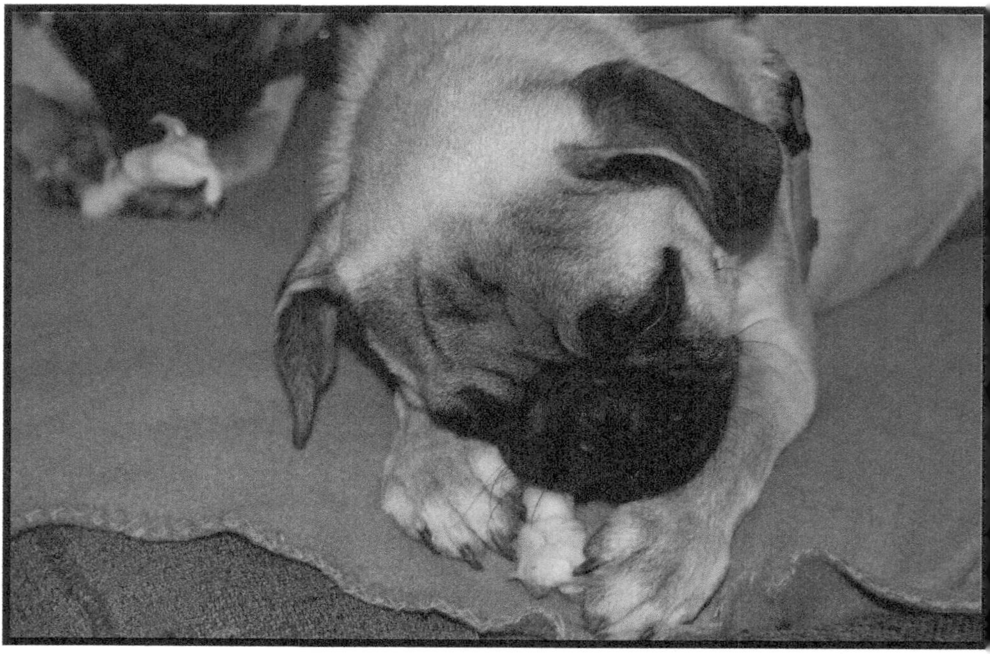

Chapter 13
The Treat Pirate

"He knew and remembered exactly where he had stashed each and every one."

Doggie treats are a big deal at our house. At any given time, Diane would have bags, boxes, jars, bottles, tubes, cans, bins, pouches, and bubble packages of goodies for that perfect reward or surprise. Max could go days without consuming any real food, and as a puppy, he could devour a munchy stick in mere seconds. And Diane and I loved Max's paws. We loved watching him eat his many treats over the years and how he maneuvered his paws to do so. Curiously, while he would almost never allow me to hold one of his paws, he would always let Diane.

Since Rikah was such an agonizing nibbler, seemingly taking hours to consume even the smallest of canine delicacies, Max would often attempt, with great success, to take hers during the process. I'm sure Rikah let him do it because she favored Max. He was her boy. We would always give her another, so there was nothing for her to worry about. She could recommence her laborious positioning, nibbling, and licking. But this also meant Max had gotten two treats, which was all part of his master plan. Sometimes, he'd bury the extra in the house somewhere for later. Some people have junkyard dogs; we have junk food dogs.

It took Diane and me some time to come up with dog treats Max liked, but once he was hooked, he couldn't get enough. Just like all puppies, Max had perfected his own brand of naughtiness, and we would entice him to act respectful using treats as an incentive. But we consistently used them in the wrong way, reinforcing his bad behavior. Although, as I've said before, Max was never really bad—just naughty. Perhaps he was bad in the eyes of others, but with us being "bad parents," we thought his behavior was nothing other than cute. After a protracted period of calling him, chasing him, or searching for him, he would either magically appear or allow us to catch him just for a treat. Which, of course, we would give him. Bad behavior reinforced. Smarter than us, he would consistently use this tactic to get rewarded.

Max also loved the longer-lasting treats such as rawhide rings or sticks that generally couldn't be consumed in a single sitting. They came with their own set of problems. Max would take one, chew it for a while, then run off with it to another part of the house. We just thought he wanted some privacy to enjoy his doggie delicacy. We'd forget we even gave him one. The next day, he'd want another. A few days would go by, and Max would show up in the den with a treat in his mouth.

"Did you give that to Max?" I'd ask Diane.

She'd shake her head. "No. I thought you did."

Although mystified, we wouldn't give it too much of a second thought.

One day, when Diane was deep cleaning the house, she walked into the living room holding five or six partially eaten treats and handed them to me.

"Look what I found!" she said.

"Where did those come from?" I asked.

"I found them in the couch, under rugs, and behind pillows." She laughed.

Well, mystery solved. Max was hiding his unfinished treats all over the house then digging them up when he wanted one. From that point forward, Diane would confiscate them when she was cleaning, and it would completely ruin Max's game. We'd find him furiously digging between the couch cushions to find a treat he had recently buried, and when he couldn't locate it, he'd look up at us in confusion, wondering why it wasn't there. I can't remember ever laughing harder. And it wasn't just random. He knew and remembered exactly where he had stashed each and every one. It was almost as if he had a doggie treat treasure map. Sometimes, he would dig up one Diane missed during the cleaning process. Nothing would make Max prouder than reuniting with a treat we had overlooked.

Me and Max

Chapter 14
Max the Ambassador

"More than once, I had to pull him away from his newfound friends before things got ugly..."

It didn't take much to get Max to go on a road trip, which oftentimes included shopping. "Go for a ride, Max?" He would leap off the couch eager to go, but getting him leashed up in his harness was always a challenge. He was such a good car companion, and he loved to meet people wherever we went, so I tried to take him with me all the time, and he would sulk if I overlooked him. For occasions when I couldn't, I would say, "Next time, Max." If you think he wouldn't remember, think again. The very next time he would see me approach the exit door with my car keys, he would anxiously stare me down to see if I was going to keep my promise.

Max would consistently embarrass me in all the stores I would take him to, sometimes two or three on a given trip. Most of the stores kept doggie treats on hand at the checkout counters, and it soon became obvious Max's picky eating habits didn't end with dog food. Observing Max's friendliness, the checkout person would reach under the counter for a treat and offer it to him. Max would look at it, sniff it, then turn up his nose and look away with a "how- could-you-ever-expect-me-to-eat-something-like-that" look on his face. Sometimes, he would add his trademarked head shake. And it wasn't a short and quick process. It was almost as if he liked to prolong my embarrassment with a ten or fifteen second evaluation and rejection period. Always a first sniff, then maybe a second, combined with perhaps a tentative lick, then followed quickly by the inevitable head shak rejection. Other times, he would take the treat, walk three steps, drop it on the floor and walk away. That was even worse because now the place had a treat they couldn't give to somebody else's dog.

Eventually, I stopped allowing him to embarrass me, short-circuiting the process by embarrassing myself first with a preemptive "no, thank you" followed by a wandering explanation that only made sense if you had a dog. I would explain how I cooked for him, how we fed him human food, and how long it took for me to find ready-made treats he actually liked. Blah, blah, blah. The counter people would tune out about halfway through since the line behind me inevitably began to get long, and they had a job to do.

This sequence of events provided the proverbial gold mine for Max. As the lin lengthened, my longwinded explanation simply gave Max more time to make friends with all the people behind me. He would work the line, starting with anyone who would acknowledge him. Max would look up at any interested party with excitement, his tail wagging frantically and a smirk plastered on his face. People would reach down and pet his head, and he'd pant loudly in response. Scratch him behind the ears, and he'd be your best friend. Strangers just loved him. He'd also make sure I saw him, looking over at me with a satisfied, happy-dog look, almost as if he wanted me to see how popular he was. What a diva. More than once, I had to pull him away from his newfound friends before things got ugly because Max was single-handedly holding up any possible progress in the store.

It was clear, according to Max, the more people who liked him the better. He loved people, the attention, and being the center of the universe. Whenever I returned to the store without Max, the salespeople would ask why I left him home. Diane and I always thought Rikah was the diva of our four-legged group, but no, it was clearly Max.

Puppy Jaxon under a giant Max

Chapter 15
Go, Max, Go!

"Max is so fast!"

Max was also a show-off. He and Jaxon would constantly compete for attention. When we focused on one dog more than the other, the ignored dog would attempt to recapture the spotlight. But they did that in different ways. Jaxon loved to play "gimme dat," which was a game where I would taunt him with a toy, and he'd try to take it away from me. Max never joined in. Apparently, my silly contest was beneath him. But if I engaged in the activity for too long, he'd feel left out, and he would jump off the couch, stand at our square coffee table, and stare me down.

"Go, Max, go!" I'd yell. He would then run around the coffee table in counterclockwise circles so the entire place would notice and egg him on.

"Faster, Max, faster!" I'd say.

Max would respond by going just a bit faster.

"Max is so fast!" Diane would echo. And he couldn't get enough of the attention.

Of course, if Max was the initiator of the ruckus, Jaxon would feel slighted, and he'd run to a get another toy to play "gimme dat." Standing on the sidelines, Rikah and Zoe would bark at us, making the place a true doggie madhouse.

I often remarked to Diane that if someone told me when we built our house in 1999 it would become a place where six crazy dogs would be living, I would have told them they were the crazy one. But that was the essence of rescuing. To transform beings who had no hope, no security, and nothing to look forward to into life-loving creatures. Dogs, in particular, just want to be happy. They want to love. And they will love you no matter what. I'm glad we could put our house to such good use.

Chapter 16

Max the German Shepherd?

"...Pugs don't do this stuff"

After four months with us, Max weighed almost fourteen pounds, a far cry from the clumsy, frightened, giant-pawed puppy we had taken home back in January. He was filling out, but he was far from turning into a pug-fat Pillsbury Doughboy. I remember wondering often what breed of dog he really was. His shape resembled that of a larger dog breed, a "real dog," as I liked to call them. His snout was much more pronounced than that of a pug. He had a giant mouth and tongue, and he was taller and more streamlined than a typical rollie-pollie pug. Plus, he was comical and extremely energetic. At that point in the year, we were chasing each other around the yard every time I brought him outside.

Pugs don't do this stuff, I remember thinking to myself. Although he was classified as one by our rescuer, he just didn't act or look like a purebred. I thought maybe he had some German shepherd in him, but his fawn coat wouldn't make sense if that were the case. With my limited knowledge, I had no idea what type of mixed-breed dog we had brought home.

Max also possessed other un-pug-like traits. When we were chasing each other in the front yard, I would run hard, but he would run slightly harder—just enough to stay ahead of me. He was a puppy, and I was, well, old and getting older. I still had some breath and endurance left, but I'd often think, *I better stop, or I'm going to pass out.* When I would halt, Max would do the same. He'd turn around just out of arms reach. Then he would smile at me with his tongue hanging loose. If I even looked like I was going to start after him again, he would run a few feet and look back at me, staying just far enough away so I couldn't catch him—but close enough to make me want to.

Was he laughing at me? It certainly looked that way. It was our little game, and he loved to play it. "Let's get Max," I would say, and he'd immediately sprint away. He would only let me catch him when he wanted me to pet him or give him a treat.

In contrast to Rikah, Max never bit as a puppy, even playfully. I had to tease him hard to provoke a light bite from him, and even then, I could see it was done with reluctance. Essentially, it was him just resting his teeth on my hand. Just like his heart, Max was the gentlest of dogs. Whenever I would put my face close to Max's, he would lick my nose and smile. Every time. "Give me a kiss, Max," I would say. All this just added to my confusion since none of our true pugs would do the same.

In contrast to the standard pug persona, Max could not get enough of going out. Whenever I would say, "Wanna go out?" to the group, he was always the first in line. And the last back in. Rain, snow, hurricanes. It didn't matter. He'd come back in the house soaking with precipitation and vigorously shake himself off, making a mess. Thinking further, he probably did it deliberately just for a little attention from the dry off. But it never mattered to me. For him to be alive, happy, and loving the excitement of each day was all I wanted for him. I'd dry him off with a giant towel and a few minutes later, he'd want to go out again.

Diane remembers the first time she had to take Max and Rikah to go somewhere. Max jumped right up into the car, while Rikah threw a fit and refused to get in. She said it was a real wrestling match to get her in the car. Diane recounted the short histories of our two puppies and what she reasoned made sense. Max was saved by a car, and in any case, he just wanted to have fun. Cars were good, and car rides were fun. From Rikah's perspective, on the other hand, every time a car showed up, she would summarily be carted off to a new place. Four of them. No wonder she didn't want to go. She had found her forever home, and she wanted to stay, so cars were bad. Although we had previously read during our puppy research dogs have a short memory span, it certainly didn't seem to be the case with either of them.

Max was a constant problem during our frequent walks with the entire pack. Although it wasn't such an issue when we had just him and Rikah, a four-dog walk added a different dimension to the dynamic. While Rikah would occasionally dart off if she saw a potential threat to the group, or if she wanted to explore something outside of our usual route, she and the twins would generally stay in formation. Being so singularly focused on leading, she made sure her troops knew she was in charge and would rarely allow herself to break from that role. The formation was Rikah to my right and in the lead, Zoe just behind but next to Rikah, and Max somewhere in front of me but to the right and behind those two. For some reason, Jaxon preferred to walk to my left and so close to me I would almost trip over him or his leash. I would try to switch him over to the main group, but sometimes he'd stay, and sometimes he wouldn't. And it wasn't easy to make the move while handling the other briskly walking critters.

One of Max's peculiarities was he loved to walk in circles. Constantly. And always counterclockwise. This was one of his primary means of communication. He would do it vigorously if he got excited. Like when I'd ask if he wanted to go out. Or if he wanted his favorite treat. Or dinner. Or anything else he really wanted to do. "Do you have to go pee-pee, Max?" The velocity and diameter of his circling would depend upon the urgency of his need or the accuracy of my question. In time, Diane and I were able to predict with some level of precision exactly what Max wanted and how badly.

But his circling carried over to other aspects of Max's daily activities, which brings me back to the walk issue. For reasons unknown, Max would unpredictably and with some frequency in the middle of a walk commence a wide, counterclockwise circle around the entire group. This would throw the entire formation into utter chaos. One minute, he'd be trotting along in pace, and the next we'd all be caught in a web of leashes. More than once, I had to stop and untangle myself from the wound-up dogs who were attempting to flee in different directions. But they were still tethered to me, their fearless leader. It would take me five minutes to get myself unwrapped and everyone reorganized only to have Max do the same exact thing twenty feet later. Once they had me tied up so effectively I fell flat on my face in the driveway. I eventually got smart, and as soon as I saw Max start to break formation, I would switch his leash to the other hand, follow him all the way around, and we'd wind up where we started, more or less. It was a delicate balancing act with the group still moving, but I was able to pull it off more often than not.

None of the other pugs made loops, which only added to my confusion about what breeds Max had in him. Interestingly, Max was a great one-on-one walker and never circled when it was only me and him. Go figure. He would stay on course and walk for as long and as far as I could. He loved it, and I would tell people Max would walk to California if somebody would take him.

To say Max was high maintenance would be somewhat of an understatement. Sometimes, if I was sitting on the couch, Max would come over with one of his large treats. If I attempted to help him up on the couch, he'd drop the treat before being lifted. I'd then need to retrieve it and hand it back to him before the other dogs stole it. While he would sometimes jump up himself, he always preferred to be lifted like a king to his throne. He relished the attention.

Still, the breed question loomed. Diane took the dogs to a doggie day at one of the parks, and someone there asked the revealing question, "Where did you get the boxer?"

Hmmm, a boxer. I hadn't thought of that one.

The timing of the question happened to coincide with my annual trip to upstate New York for a model airplane event, and the campground owner had a mid-sized boxer he'd let run free around the site during the event. I took careful notice of the dog's antics over the four or five days I was there. Similar physique. Check. Protruding snout. Check. Giant tongue hanging out of one side of the mouth. Check. Giant smile. Check. Playful but gentle demeanor. Check. Sensitive to loud noises. Check. Would run a few yards and then stop, turn around, and look back at you. Check. Likes to explore. Check.

Things were starting to add up, but then I saw something that sealed the deal He circled for no apparent reason. I almost couldn't believe it. Max had some boxe in him. The similarities between the two dogs were shocking—only the colors anc sizes were different. After doing a bit of internet research, Diane and I conclude boxers were gentle, friendly, and exploring dogs just like Max.

Max was a pug/boxer, otherwise known as a "bug."

Even we couldn't tell them apart

Chapter 17
Zoe and Jaxon

"They are inseparable."

About a year after we got Max, Zoe and Jaxon, a brother and sister pair of pure, 100 percent pugs got on our radar. They were in Vermont, and their pregnant mother had been rescued from an Ohio puppy mill. Their rescuers were searching for a home for them and contacted us since the rescue circles are small, and everyone by then knew of Diane's letter.

Aside from Jaxon having some white markings on his chin, we couldn't tell them apart. As such, to this day, Zoe and Jaxon are known as "the twins." They were part of an original litter of three, two boys and a girl, but we felt we could only take two at the time, which in retrospect, was a mistake. Seeing over the years how much the twins love and interact with each other, we have always felt it was a shame we didn't take the third. They are inseparable. They communicate with each other. They welcome each other with sniffs, kisses, and hugs when they have been apart, regardless of the timespan.

While their mother had been a puppy mill inhabitant, the trio was born under the protection of the rescuers, so their situation was quite different from Rikah's and Max's. They needed a permanent home, and of course, it was February and snowy when we agreed to take the two needy additions. This meant a trip to Vermont, the very place you shouldn't go during the winter unless you like to ski.

The drive that day was quite challenging. It began to sleet and snow ten minutes into the trip and didn't stop until we reached Pennsylvania on the return leg. Since our current dogs, Rikah and Max, were still puppies, we couldn't leave them home for what amounted to a full day, so we brought them with us. While the SUV we had was well equipped for the weather and the passengers, it was still a stressful trip. But Max just loved being in a car and with the family. With Diane and Rikah in the back, Max hung out on the seat next to me. It was all just fun to him. A new adventure. Each time the conditions and traffic would stress me out, I'd look over at smiley Max and then everything would be okay.

Jaxon is noticeably the brighter of the two and is hysterically naughty and stubborn. Zoe is a quintessential pleaser who hangs on our every request and always tries to do the right thing. I can always count on Zoe to come in when I call her.

Of the group, Zoe has the greatest number of nicknames (visit the back of this book for a comprehensive list), and she answers to them all. Opening the floodgate for Zoe was Diane's niece, Mikala, who yelled "Zo-Zo" when she was helping me bring the dogs in from a protracted outing. Zoe came running. The grandkids added a few more since at the time, they couldn't pronounce anything with a "Z" in it. "Jo-Jo, Jo-Jo" was often heard from them, and Zoe, nevertheless, still came running. Since Zoe likes to eat, and as a result, began to resemble a polar bear, I started the whole "Zoe Bear" thing. This name morphed into "Zo-Zo Bear" and then, of course, to "Jo-Jo Bear." To Zoe, all these names are terms of endearment and she loves to be summoned with any of them. Probably because she thinks there's food waiting for her upon her arrival. And okay, there usually is.

One of Zoe's unfortunate traits is she gets car sick. We discovered this on day one when she vomited the entire car ride home from Vermont to Pennsylvania. I found out later if I calmed her by petting her head, it takes her mind off the ride and reduces the chances of her getting sick. But then she insists on sitting on my lap in the car, looking out the window while I'm driving. It's funny when I pull up at a traffic light and people notice the pug looking out the window. She will then start barking when she notices the people.

Jaxon has become rather infamous over the years for his uncanny ability to steal treats and human food. We call him "Recon" since he just simply finds the way. The way to the food. I'm not really sure how much he shares with the other dogs when he finds a cache, but if you have it, he will find it.

Diane witnessed his ability firsthand after leaving a four-pack of treats in the front seat of the car while she ran into the pet store. While checking out, she peered through the window toward the car. The group was shuffling around excitedly, egging Jaxon on to undertake a critical mission. They settled down and disappeared for a few seconds, but then Jaxon popped up smartly, struggling to squeeze around the anti-dog netting we had installed in the gaps in the car. Diane had done a surprisingly good job at sealing off the treasure in the front seat, but a second try yielded success. Jax managed to climb up and over the seat, cramming himself through an incredibly tight gap near the ceiling. He immediately started in on the treat bags. At one point, he even got behind the steering wheel and looked like he was going to drive off with his booty. Diane ran to the car and promptly shut the party down, informing me later with a laugh she was glad she didn't leave the keys. True to form, none of the dogs got in trouble. In fact, I bet you they even got a few treats.

Of our six dogs, Jaxon is also the laziest. He just loves to lounge around and sit with Diane twenty-four hours a day. He doesn't really seem to mind snow or bad weather, but it's getting him there that's the issue. Even though the other dogs may already have done a pee-pee run two or three times during a given day, Jaxon just sits quietly and hopes I don't call him. He will actually hide, not moving a muscle, when I do call him, and he's a master at holding it. He is so stubborn he resists when I attempt to pick him up to join the other dogs. Deanna, our niece, says, "He makes himself heavy." And she's right. Picking up Jaxon is like picking up a twenty-pound bag of stones.

Of all of them, Jaxon is the most endearing and sensitive little pug. Unflappable and always Mr. Cool, he'll greet me when I enter a room then sit patiently for me to notice him. If I happen to overlook him, he'll either sulk or look at me intensely with the message I had somehow missed him.

Jaxon loves to watch doggie programs on the television. He loves *Dog Hotel* and the Westminster agility events. And it's not just an occasional glance at the screen. Jaxon is completely riveted by the TV. A sign of intelligence, methinks. During one of the show dog contests, we placed him on a low coffee table and then judged him as the officials do with the dogs on TV. Jaxon played the part perfectly, standing straight, still, and calmly as we evaluated his posture while positioning him and commenting to the fictitious audience. He and Zoe love to bark at the dogs on TV, and Jax will turn and look at me if I fail to fast forward through the commercials. When we happen to watch an event as it's being broadcast, it's hard to explain to him we can't do the fast forward thing.

Rikah initially treated Zoe and Jaxon as invaders. She practically gave the two assigned seating on the couch and always allowed Max to keep the primo spot between Diane and I. Rikah also doesn't like when I pet Zoe or have her sit with me. It's how I learned about dog pecking order. Of the original four, it's Rikah, Max, Jaxon, and Zoe. But this ordering makes no sense. Max, having only one good eye and a relatively timid demeanor, should have been last in the pecking order. But Rikah would have none of that. Max was Rikah's boy. So, she consistently demanded he be second, and when challenged, a fight would ensue. Jaxon is relatively apathetic to the whole issue. As long as Diane is nearby, the world is a happy place for him. If Max, who understood Rikah's intentions all too well, felt his position was being threatened, he would throw a fit. Rikah would then automatically tangle with Zoe. This was the only unfortunate side of Max's diva status among the group, bestowed upon him and maintained by the boss, Rikah. She and Max had been the top dogs for over a year, and nothing was going to change that.

The other issue at play is Zoe's personality type. We concluded she's not a very good "pack" dog. Diane and I noticed these dynamics somewhat well into her life with us. Zoe seems to be the happiest when I take her on one-on-one trips, away from the influence of the group. And while she is an affectionate and obedient dog, and funny in her own way, this mostly surfaces only when she's away from the pressure of her boss. While I feel sorry for her, I avoid contradicting or usurping Rikah's power over the group at all costs since she's such a good leader. This is a pack, Rikah's the boss, and those are the rules. Our showing Zoe more love and attention helped her deal with it, and the change in her mood each day forward was noticeable.

Totally 100 percent pug, Zoe and Jaxon are the most affectionate of dogs. My beautiful twins.

Tucky and his stick

Chapter 18
Tucker and Lola

"...it seems as if the two have been here from the beginning..."

Tucker arrived about eight years after Zoe and Jaxon. Currently a two-year-old puppy, he is so strong, fast, and active our vet has renamed him the "Bruiser." And that he is. Pick him up and he feels as solid as a cured bag of cement. And about as heavy. If I do manage to pick him up, and he's not feeling the love at the time, I won't be holding him for long. With his long body, short hair, real dog strength, constant nose to the ground sniffing, and lightning speed, we continue to doubt the claim Tucker is all pug. He has the coloring of a pug, but that is where the similarities end.

We adopted him when Diane got a call about a pug puppy who was dropped off by a breeder at a kill shelter down south. The rescuers were desperate to find a home for him since he had only a few days left to live, so Diane took him and told me about it later. I was glad she did. The story goes he was not a perfect pug, and he probably wouldn't have commanded top dollar as a breed dog, so he was thrown away. Imagine that.

He had a hernia, which we immediately took care of, and his forehead lines and facial coloring were not up to prevailing pug specifications. But make no mistake, Tuck is a handsome, intelligent dog, and he has the most orderly sit of any of our dogs. So good, in fact, he should demonstrate it to the military. I just love to watch him sit, after which he intensely looks up, waiting for my next move. But forget about him sitting for long. Like lightning, Tucker is never in the same spot twice.

While he's a typical active, rambunctious puppy, he's also a most sensitive creature and hangs on our every word. What a smartie.

I always thought one of his nicknames should've been "Sticks" since he loves to seek out and carry them. When we first got Tucker, he picked up a branch that was probably four or five feet in length during one of our walks. He was so proud strutting along with it. The stick was so large, it was practically walking him. Eventually, he started to eat them, and our house became full of chewed-up twigs. The vet, with good reason, advised us to discourage the practice, but we didn't have much success. Recently, Diane spied him in the fireplace, sitting among the ashes chewing on some wood. Tucker!

Tucker loves to run and wander, and just forget about trying to chase him. When he escapes, usually to torment the neighbors with his cacophonous bark, I simply call him and hope he eventually shows up. With him being so fast and elusive, that's just about all I can do. When I somehow get to within shouting distance, he darts off, relegating me to being only an observer. He slipped away from me unleashed at the vet's office recently, and it took the entire office staff to corral him. Doctors included.

Sometimes, when I really need him to come back, I'll choose what I call "the nuclear option." Shouting "Mommy's here!" generally does it with him and any others who happen to be straying. They all come running. Apparently, they like Mommy better. But I am careful not to push the red button too often since they, similar to the story about the boy who cried wolf, will simply get used to that particular call and summarily ignore it. Forever.

Rocket dog Tucker, in stark contrast to Zoe and Jaxon, never does anything in slow motion. Able to leap tall buildings in a single bound, another un-pug-like trait, Tucker will run and dart through the house at the slightest provocation. Toys, food, treats, visitors; Tucker is on it and fast. If I could ever train him, he would be perfect for the Westminster Dog Show agility competition. Throw a toy and Tucker will jump over seemingly impossible obstacles to chase it down, sliding and clawing his way across the floor to get it. And it doesn't matter who or what happens to be in his way at the time, including poor little unsuspecting Lola. Hence the nickname "Bam-Bam." He will barge through partially open doors at full speed when there is something on the other side he wants, causing the door to swing wildly open with a crash. He will also attempt to do so with a latched door, almost taking it off its hinges. I guess he thinks it's ajar. When he's done, his pug side takes over, and he'll sit and snuggle with Mommy and the others.

So, what is Tucker? The question looms to this day. His shape, strength, and short coat are not at all pug-like, but his coloring and his signature double-tail curl are. Neither Diane nor I can figure him out exactly. Interestingly, he is beginning to resemble Max in both his physical appearance and in the way he reacts and communicates. He also prefers to dine alone in Max's room, although he is a much less fussy eater. Diane feels a higher authority must have sent him to help us deal with our loss. Does Max's spirit reside within Tucker? I am not much of a believer in such things, but the timing, the resemblance, and the persona seem to be more than a coincidence. As a final argument in favor of this view, Tucker's tail curls to his right, just as Max's did. Hmmm.

I had met Lola's owner, Sonia, an elderly woman who also had a border collie, at the vet's office during one of my frequent trips there. She and I began discussing our pets, and she noted she was about to move into a retirement home, and the landlord would allow her to keep only a single dog. So, she was looking for a place for her twelve-year-old pug, Lola. I remember not saying much since we already had five dogs, and I felt it might be a stretch for us to take another. About a week or two passed, and our vet called Diane to advise her Sonia's family was intending to euthanize Lola since they had been unsuccessful in finding a home for her. We immediately agreed to take her.

Lola was not in the best of shape. She hadn't had her standard shots in four years, hadn't been groomed, and could barely walk since she wasn't exercised on a regular basis. Lola had infections in her paws and in her "under the nose" wrinkle, the latter of which is a standard pug issue if left unattended. When I picked her up to take her home, I noted Lola was bony and weak. I learned later she was fed only a handful of dog food per day. I thought to myself at the time, *Well, we can fix that.* While not a true rescue, she was certainly a rescue enough, and lucky little Lola was about to enter doggie paradise.

Lola's coat and nails were too long, and she was generally unkempt, so the first thing we did was get her groomed and cleaned up. A clean and brush, as I like to say. Then we took her for all her delinquent vaccinations, and the vet gave us a prescription for her infections. For the next month or so, I would clean her paws and wrinkle twice a day. Between that and the medicine, things began to get better. I also spent a lot of time petting and coddling her since she seemed to be such a nervous little thing. "Don't be scared, we'll take care of you," I would say to her each night before bed. If a bit uncertain, Lola is nevertheless the sweetest of dogs.

It took a while for Lola to respond to the new treatment and surroundings, but day by day, her tail began to rise into that happy pug curl, and she started walking with her head up. As I grew to know her, I could tell when Lola was relaxed and content. She sits next to me and licks her front paws when all is well. True to form, I followed my "food is love" equation to the letter, and Lola eats like a horse. I have never seen a dog eat with such voraciousness. She doesn't simply eat her food, she obliterates it. But spoiling her was long overdue.

As she filled out, her coat became softer, and she shed less hair. She was getting healthier and more active as a result. I fully realize she doesn't have too many years left, so my goal is to spoil her as much as possible in the meantime. Food and treats, mainly. Yes, I'm happy to have her, and if she gets fat during the process, so much the better. Food is happiness with Lola.

Although Lola was immediately accepted by the existing pug management, most likely due to her matronly status in the group, no mercy was shown to her by the pack during our outside walks. Similar to United States Marine Corps basic training, the pack expected her to walk and comingle if she wanted any kind of status among them. Although a bit shaky at first, Lola got stronger with each outing and began trailing the group wherever it went. The nice thing is, since she follows me almost exclusively, she doesn't need a leash. Admittedly, on the longer walks, I have to pick her up and carry her back when I notice her starting to lag, but she at least tries, and I love her for it. Lola is a tough little trooper.

She is prone these days to having seizures even though we have her on medicine for it. While they are sporadic, with each one she loses a little bit more of her eyesight and can now barely see anything unless it is right in front of her. Our house is a wide-open ranch with a single floor, and she sometimes gets lost, prompting me to send out a Lola "search and rescue" party. But it's usually just me playing the role of seeing eye dog. The degradation of her eyesight affected her navigation abilities, so Lola often winds up traveling in a direction exactly opposite of where she needs to go. I suppose from her perspective, the forest of table and chair legs in the kitchen look the same as those in the dining room.

The amazing thing is even Rikah accepted her, probably because of Lola's advanced age and the fact she presented little competition for the top dog spot. Motherly Rikah doesn't let Lola get too far out of her sight during our walks, and she doesn't seem to mind the additional head count. Lola only wants to eat and hang with me and that appears to be just fine with Rikah. I feel too the camaraderie of the group has been immensely helpful to Lola's health and overall happiness. While Lola sometimes snaps for good reason at overly obnoxious, "bull-in-a-China-shop" Tucker, she loves being in the group and occupying her place in the pack. Then, she'll sleep soundly in a doggie bed snuggled in with him. Go figure.

Lola and Tucker. It's both amazing and heartwarming to me to see how our original pack of four immediately accepted these two needy and unsure newcomers, even with each of them being at the opposite ends of the age and personality spectrums. So much so it seems as if the two have been here from the beginning as we observed them settle into the group and become accustomed to our crazy, dog-house routines.

I have come to realize dogs are almost human-like, with each having their own unique needs, dreams, and personalities. As I watch Lola and Tucker happily interact with our original four, I wish I could take in all who need a home. Perhaps another hundred would be about right. I think so.

Max looks surprisingly happy here

Chapter 19

Dress-up Day

"The experiment didn't last long, which was actually a blessing in disguise."

For some unknown reason, when Rikah and Max were relatively young, Diane insisted on dressing them both up for photo shoots, holidays, social gatherings, and even minor events. Sometimes, no occasion was needed at all. Rikah loved it. She'd prance around like a super model on a runway. Long scarves were her favorite. Wrap her up in one, and she'd become a movie star on awards night. Max, on the other hand, hated it. Put a costume on him and Max would sulk and attempt to hide. I felt sorry for him. While he liked wearing his collegiate sweaters during the winter, he seriously disliked the silly outfits. And believe me, he knew the difference. My goal was always to make Max happy, not humiliate him, so for that reason, I hated dress-up day too.

Of all the outfits Diane could and would conjure for the pair, and there were many, the absolute worst were those she had selected for our annual Oktoberfest party. Rikah, as usual, didn't mind a bit, but Max had a real problem with his. It came with the hat and all the associated Teutonic accouterments. "Extra silly," I would say. There was no way I would have donned anything that moronic, and it appeared Max felt the same way. I had no idea she had dressed up Max in such a costume, otherwise I'd have shut the proceedings down before they had even gotten started.

With everyone outside on a beautiful fall day, making noise and enjoying the German music and food, Max refused to mingle, preferring instead to sit on the couch in the den and sulk. When Max didn't want to go outside and meet people, I knew there was a problem. As soon as I saw his predicament, I immediately extricated him from the ridiculous outfit. His reaction was almost as if I had thrown a light switch. Maxie instantaneously brightened up, jumped off the couch, and joined the party outside, wagging his tail. Who knew dogs could sense such a difference when it came to what they were wearing?

Rikah had her moments also. If we dress her in anything not fashion-related, such as foul weather gear, or if the garment in question does not meet her high standards of color, we're in big trouble. Orange, in particular, is a no-no. As a result, Diane's ridiculous Halloween outfit was used only once. Of course, I will again blame Diane for her overly enthusiastic inclinations when it came to protecting our dogs in bad or cold weather. While the intention was certainly honorable, Rikah detests foul weather gear in any form. Probably because to her, it's a sign of weakness, and in any case, none of it is fashionable. Especially the dog-specific stuff.

In one instance, Diane had gotten puppy Rikah a horrible, blazing-yellow vinyl raincoat, replete with a stretchy hood and four matching little doggie booties. The only thing missing were the words "Police" or "Road Crew" on the back. The experiment didn't last long, which was actually a blessing in disguise. While the both of us were attempting to get the booties on each of her tiny paws one rainy day, Rikah was already tearing the flimsy raincoat to shreds. Aside from immediately flinging the booties off her paws one by one as we laboriously managed to get each of them on, we were also the recipients of a huff-and-puff Rikah lecture, advising us not to ever try something like that again.

The blessing was there was no way I was going to continue to spend twenty minutes dressing up a crazy little dog just so she could go outside for a pee in the rain. *Go ahead,* I thought. *Get wet. Be my guest.* And that's exactly what she did. As I watched her venture outside into the weather that day, I could almost hear her say, "I'll show you. I don't need no stinkin' raincoat." If I know Rikah, she cared more about making her point than she did about getting wet.

Even the twins have their own oddities. Neither Zoe nor Jaxon like to wear anything at any time for warmth, fashion, bad weather, or the cold. Nothing. Put a sweater or an outfit on either of them, and they will freak out and run through the house, trying to get it off. A transformation not unlike Dr. Jekyll and Mr. Hyde.

Sweet and lovable little Lola, however, loves anything provided to her as long as I'm the one providing it. She is perpetually cold, and it's a lot colder in the house at the lower altitudes where she spends most of her time. So, for three quarters of the year, I put a sweater on her, but she appears to be the most comfortable with the same one each time. Tucker? High speed, low drag Tucker doesn't seem to require any kind of gear whatsoever, and we've never attempted to dress him up. I presume he wouldn't want anything extra that would slow him down.

With six dogs at one point, it became a challenge to understand who does what, who wants what, and who doesn't like what. To tone down the complexity, we really need some kind of master doggie chart to track all the dos and don'ts for each of them. It takes hours to explain everything to a dog sitter the two times a year Diane and I venture out to do something without the pack. Perhaps that's the reason we never had the same sitter twice.

Tucker the punk

Chapter 20
Our Four-Legged Amphibians

"For a half second, I stood there, dumbfounded."

I often say to Diane the good news is we have a pool. The bad news? That we have a pool. Since complaining appears to be an incorrigible part of my personality, during the years before having the dogs, I would continually make snarky remarks about the amount of care and maintenance the pool requires. But since we live in an area having four seasons, my wife would generally be subject to my whining only for a couple of months each year. The acquisition of our dogs, however, changed all that. Like a fine wine, my dislike of the pool has gradually aged into a full-time, extreme hatred, to put it mildly. Companies insuring homes against liability classify pools as an "attractive nuisance," an apt description when it comes to dogs. They walk up to it, they walk too close to it, and sometimes, they walk into it.

Pugs, I discovered, float about as well as a streamlined crowbar with lead sinkers attached, and so I cannot, under any circumstances, simply let them out by themselves to do their business when the pool is open. And during the off season, when the pool is closed and covered with a giant, expensive, and flexible purpose-built tarp, Tucker uses it as a doggie trampoline, his own private playground. Moreover, being the smart-assed wise guy he is, he learned very quickly I cannot follow him on it or chase him off it. That little punk. He continually runs across it when I chase him, playfully splashing around in the water that comes up through its porous surface, and he does so regardless of the ambient air temperature. It actually looks like fun to me. But he's still a punk.

In my view, the pool is a true dog hazard, and more than once, I've had a couple of them inadvertently slip in or in one case, actually jump into it unwittingly. Rikah and Max were the only ones not to experience the official "falling in the pool" initiation at the rescue house. Retrospectively, I suppose these incidents were humorous, but at the time, they were anything but. Zoe, in particular, has gone for a few unintended swims in the pool. She couldn't have been more than a year old when she was lollygagging along and playfully interacting with her brother, Jaxon, but doing so exceedingly close to the pool's slippery edge. In she went. Fortunately, I was walking immediately behind them, almost expecting it to happen, and scooped her out before she realized she had gone in. A similar event occurred years later with sweet little Lola. Unfazed, Lola never missed a beat as I restored her to terra firma.

Not long after her first dip, a fattened-up Zoe unexpectedly went in again, but it was probably more of my own fault. It was a late night in August, and the four dogs were dillydallying around, despite my typically loud "go pee" calls. Well, sleepy Zoe overreacted to the ferocity and volume of my order and leaped dead center into the deep end of the pool. For a half second, I stood there dumbfounded. *Did that just happen?* I took a fully clothed jump into the pool and caught up to her in seconds as she was paddling like mad with only her nose poking out of the water. I thrust her out of the pool, and I could see her eyes were as wide as saucers as she landed on its edge in a watery splat. She felt as wet as a janitor's mop as I wrapped her in a towel, telling her it was all right as I attempted to calm us both down. Diane added the exclamation point to this episode when I came inside with a sopping wet dog to tell her what had happened. "Is it raining?" she asked. It was another dog learning lesson for me. I would never use a loud tone with them ever again. Especially in the general vicinity of the open pool.

In contrast to his sister, Jaxon is a natural swimmer and a consistent "pool dog." He just loves the pool. Hold him over the water as he's about to go in, and he'll begin the doggie paddle with his paws. We have him wear a doggie life jacket—the only garment he does not attempt to shed—and he will swim around the entire pool on his own, closely supervised, of course. The laziest of lazy pugs, he will also lounge in the sun on a floating raft for hours. His inclinations are a bit of a double-edged sword as he will sometimes attempt to enter the pool all by himself with no jacket. Especially if it is a warm day. But at least he listens when I tell him a carefully toned "no."

Rikah tolerates the pool only if she is held, but her body language would seem to indicate she'd rather be sitting on dry land in a supervisory capacity. Kind of like a doggie lifeguard. For both Rikah and Lola, I use the pool only to cool them off dousing them as they sit beside it on a hot day. To me, this is a pool's only useful purpose since pugs cannot shed the heat of the summer sun.

And now, of course, I will get to Max. Max liked to be carried around in the pool to cool off and be part of the group, but he was very tentative about his entry. The following is an abridged version of Max's thought process before actually getting into the pool.

Wow! Look at everybody. That looks like fun! Then he'd sniff the pool water. *Oh, but maybe I'd better not*, he'd think, backing up from the edge.

But I don't want to be left out. Even all the kids are in! He'd run to the other side of the pool only to be hit by a splash of cold water. *Hmm. No. I don't think so.*

As he watched the kids playing, he'd change his mind again. *Okay, I'll try it. I'll just do what they're doing.* Then he'd step closer to the water to see how deep it was. *Nope, not looking good. But how about over there?*

Running to the shallow end, he'd scope it out. *Umm, no, I think I'll stay here.* Then a few seconds later, he'd think, *But the kids are having so much fun!* So, he'd run back to the other end, practically leaping in excitement. *Okay, yep. I'm good to go.* Only then he'd see his reflection. *Nope. Wait. Better not.*

Ultimately, his curiosity would get the better of him. *Okay, I'll try it. Just this once.*

It took a life jacket and three people already in the pool to coax Max to go in along with a lot of calls to "Come on, Maxie!" And he would absolutely, positively not want to get his head wet. But once he was in and being attended to by everybody, he seemed to like the pool or at least the undivided attention he was getting. I glanced back at him once while he was being carried around and saw him with his lips tightly closed and his cheeks bulging out. Max must have observed the little kids in the pool holding their breath, and he appeared to be imitating them. It was hysterical. How he learned to do that or what purpose he thought it served, I will never know.

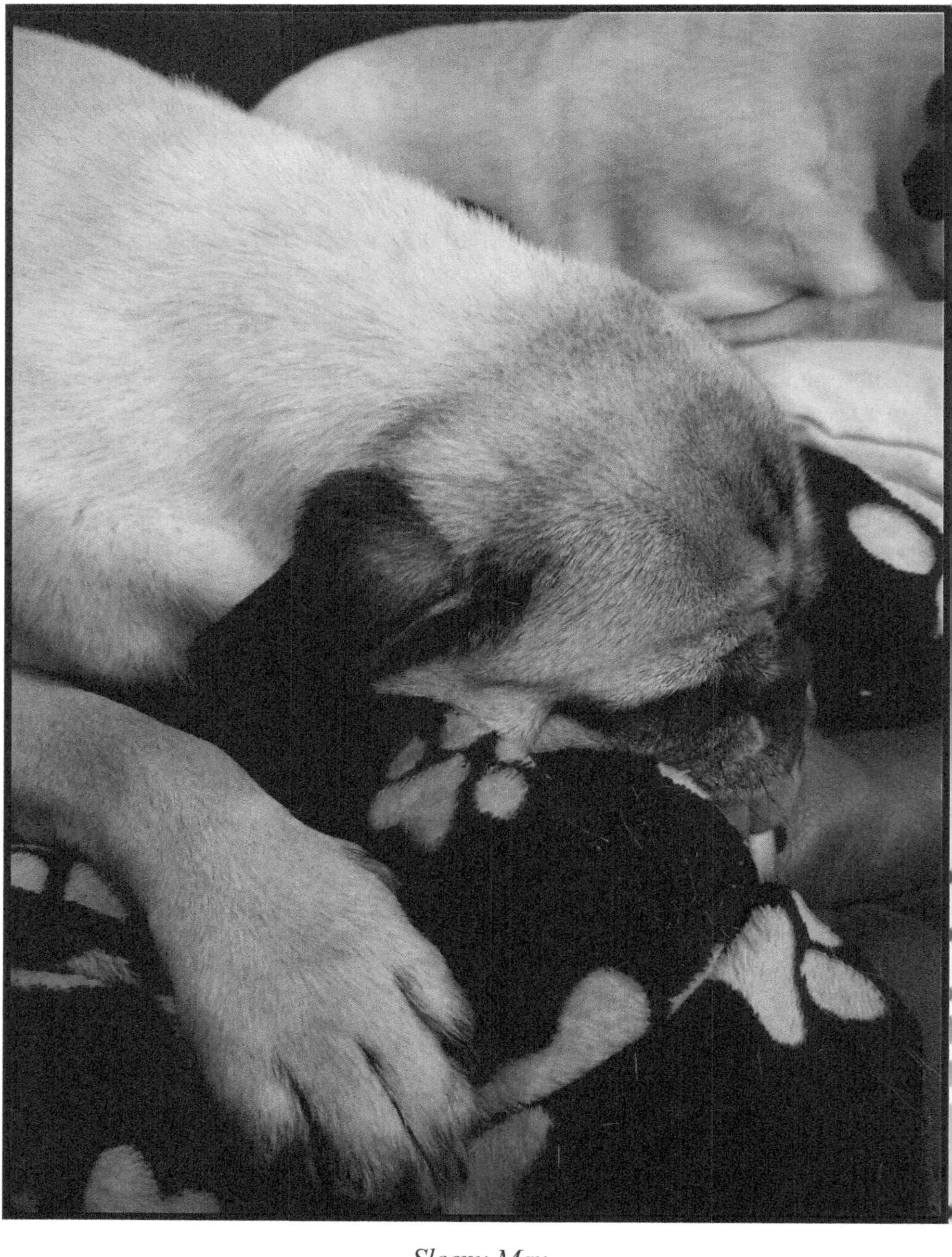

Sleepy Max

Chapter 21
The Nightly Ritual

"I learned never to break from routine with these guys."

Getting six dogs to go to bed each night was rather complicated at the rescue house. Of course, the root of the complication was the fawning attention bestowed upon the group by us, the caretakers. Once the detailed routine was established, the dogs insisted it be followed to the letter. Any variation in—or the omission of—any of its critical particulars would be followed by huffs, barks, stares, sad looks, sulks, or whines. Sometimes, a combination of all of the above would ensue, depending upon the severity of the deviation. But all was only after we actually got them up onto the bed, which in and of itself was an accomplishment.

The process would commence with an announcement by the leadership. "Wanna go to bed?" Max, and later Tucker, would immediately leap from the couch, but the other four would often display differing levels of excitement, or in the case of elderly Lola, not hear the question at all. Due to her age, she could not jump from the couch and had to be gently awakened and manually lowered to the floor. If I somehow overlooked her or let her continue to nap instead of taking her outside, she'd immediately wake up and run to the edge of the couch, barking her head off with what has to be the loudest bark ever for a little dog. Or any dog, for that matter. It has to be heard to be believed, although it's not necessarily the volume. It's the frequency. I can hear it from outside when she has been left in the house, and as a result, I have considered taping the windows with a giant "X," lest they all explode in a shower of vibrating glass.

Once everybody was on the floor, some would try to short circuit the process by heading to the hallway door, which leads to the bedroom. I guess it was okay for them to change the procedure, but not us. "No, we have to go outside to pee first," I would explain. Depending upon the outside temperature, that recommendation was met with varying levels of excitement, with a few slowly walking toward the door while the others stayed put. Sometimes, no one would go. Max and Tucker would be chomping at the bit to go out, presumably to get in the last expedition of the day. "Maybe we can get into trouble one more time!" I think that was the idea.

Zoe and Jaxon are not only the laziest and most stubborn group members, but they have also perfected the ability to hold it to almost an art form. Calling them to go out while they are snuggled on the couch is usually met with apathetic looks, clearly hoping I didn't mean it and I would just go away. Rikah is similarly reluctant, and since she didn't issue the command, she apparently doesn't feel she has to follow mine. On the other hand, if she has to go, and I'm sitting down, I had better get up and take her out. Immediately.

Once I had them all outside, the challenge was to get them to do their business. "Pee-pee, let's go pee-pee!" I would repeat over and over until something happened. It's how I finally learned the origin of the phrase "pissing contest." They would all stand around looking at each other, waiting for that first one to take a pee. The first one to blink. Once that happened, the rest would pee on top of that. And then the first one to pee would go again and pee on top of all the rest, restarting the process. I think each of them deliberately saves some so they can be the absolute last in the contest. The "winner" in doggie logic.

With six dogs, it was common to get them all to come back inside and settled for bed after the initial run only for one or two to have to do what they missed the first time. Back to "go," in other words. I always try to keep track of who has done what during the initial outing, but with six dogs, it's next to impossible. And since they all tend to go their separate ways during the process, it's difficult to tell who's who and who's doing what in the pitch black. It's especially complicated to keep track of what each may be doing two or three times. So, with the utter chaos, I take what I can get.

If it could be said Max was annoying to watch eat, his required outside pee visits were even more so. And I could never discern between a true necessity and a social visit. While I generally didn't care how long it all took in nice weather, supervising his bathroom habits during the cold was downright maddening. A snowy January night seemed to have virtually no influence upon amount of time he required to get the job done. The root of my frustration centered around his relentless circling, complicated further by the universal dog inclination to find that perfect spot. The number of conditions that had to be met for Max to have a successful pee outing must have approached those needed by NASA for an accurate moon launch.

While he certainly was an active participant in the pissing contest craziness, inevitably he would search for his own spot. And search. And search. Finally, he would appear to have one lined up and start circling to zero in on it. Then he would hear a noise from the woods or be distracted by the other dogs. He would stop, look around for the source of the distraction, and then look at me to see if I was monitoring the situation. I would tell him once again, more firmly this time, to "go pee." Only then would he recommence the search and circle process. I could never tell exactly what he was looking for or what the attributes of a perfect pee spot were. I just had to wait until it was over. And I couldn't tell him to hurry up since it amounted to an additional distraction and would delay the process even further. Keep in mind this routine was not a once-in-a-while thing; it was every time he had to go out.

Due to the time it took Max to complete the mission, the rest of the dogs were usually clustered in front of the door, milling around, anxiously waiting for me to let them back in. Especially if it was a cold night. In the interest of expediency, and since I was usually frozen by this point also, I'd often take a head count instead of attempting to identify exactly who was who. In all the confusion, some of them could still be missing in action. So, I had to be careful.

During a cold and snowy night, I had to track down Diane's son Jared's dog, Lilly, an older dog who got snowed in with us for a few days. Not the greatest of navigators, she was still outside when everyone else was already inside warming up. When the snow got deep, I'd carve a circuitous "doggie luge" around the backyard to provide the group with a well-optioned place to pee. For the most part, it began and ended at the same spot. But it was a long way around, especially for a little dog.

Well, that particular night, the snow was high and blowing, and a confused Lilly had inadvertently started a slow and laborious trek the wrong way around the luge after doing her business. *Where the heck is Lilly? There's only so many places she could go,* I thought to myself. I grabbed the flashlight and hiked just about the entire length of the luge, eventually happening upon her from behind. She was slogging it out, moving forward ever so slowly, clearly wondering where she was in the featureless trench and if she would ever get there, wherever that was. Although mostly deaf, she finally heard me calling. I couldn't have been more than three or four feet away. She turned around with the biggest dog smile I had ever seen. *I'm saved!* she had to be thinking. I whisked her back to the warmth of the den. She was a cold little dog but a happy one. Nobody gets left behind.

I could see the excitement of the pack rise when Max would come trotting back to the group, usually with a very serious look on his face. Getting back inside meant sleepy time and that meant treats.

After everybody got in, there were two more obstacles—the door into the den and another at the bedroom hallway. To enhance their excitement, I would ask, "Are you ready for bed?" All except Max would then rush to the den door, thus preventing me from opening it. "A pug jam" is what I would call it. Max would be doing his frantic excitement circles and would be last when I managed to get the door open.

Sometimes I had stupidly left it open, which would result in utter chaos since I would have to chase the six escapees all over the house. Then it was a reenactment of the "The Charge of the Light Brigade" as the group ran through the house, full speed, to the final obstacle—the hallway door. This would be blocked by even crazier dogs since they knew they were almost there. Once this last door was opened, the dogs had finally made it: treat time. Barking and yelling, they would again run full speed, slipping and sliding down the hallway to the bedroom.

Since we had four of them for a longer period than the latter two, Tucker and Lola, the process has somewhat evolved over time. The original four would run into the bedroom and three of them—Rikah, Jaxon, and Zoe—would immediately jump up on the bed, using a small bench-like armoire as a stepping-stone. No problem. These days, Tucker, the strong-as-an-ox two year old, makes it to the bed in a single leap, armoire or not, whereas twelve-year-old Lola requires a careful pick up.

Max, on the other hand, would stop in his tracks at the armoire and look at me. I know he had a bad eye, but he constantly played this unfortunate trait to his maximum advantage to get me to pick him up. "Come on, you can make it!" I would say. "You made it last night!" Only then would he try to jump up on the step and then onto the bed. This heroic effort would consist of him spinning his wheels on the slippery wood floor to gain enough forward velocity to attempt a jump. It was really hard for me not to laugh. If he didn't get enough traction, he would stop short and look at me. "Come on, Max, you can do it!" I would say again. He would try and usually make it. Very infrequently, he wouldn't make it at all and crash into the armoire. Of course, I would feel sorry for him and pick him up. But the following night he'd use that against me and want to be picked up. He would look at his objective and then back at me with sad dog eyes. I could never tell if he truly couldn't make it or if he was playing me so he wouldn't have to try the next night.

Once all four were up on the bed, things got complicated. Max insisted on having a drink of water before he went to bed. The others would feel left out whether they really wanted one or not, so I had to get them all drinks. Four cups, requiring two trips. Max and Rikah first followed by Jaxon and Zoe. Not being very smart, I served them full cups at first, thus necessitating another trip outside about a half hour later after everybody was settled, including me. Realizing this could go on all night, I later got them half cups or less.

And they each had their own way of letting me know they had to go out again. The twins would jump off the bed and wait at the door. Most of the time, I heard them do this. Rikah would do her typical huff and puff. Max was different. He would get close to my face and stare me down with the most intense look. How this woke me up I will never know, but it always did. It was almost scary. "Do you have to go out, Max?" He would respond with a few excited circles on the bed, waking everyone else up. After taking him outside, either the pee-pee process would recommence or maybe instead some midnight exploration. Although after-bedtime outings were prohibited, sometimes I think he simply wanted to explore without the distraction of the other dogs. I could never determine his intent until we got outside, but I couldn't take the chance.

Once the water had been served, it was treat time. Max, beyond happy at that point, would start to drool. I'd grab the bag, tell the dogs to sit, and offer each one a goodie, usually starting with Rikah since she was the leader. She never sat, but I allowed that given her rank. "Rikah doesn't have to sit. Rikah's the boss," I would declare so everybody understood. But the rest of them had to sit, and they did, even Max. It was hysterical watching them all try to stay, attempting to quell their enthusiasm. Some of them got so anxious they would inadvertently slip off the bed. Then everyone would bark and get agitated until the entire pack was reunited and the treats were served.

Sometimes, it would be really late when I went to bed, and I was tired, so I would erroneously think I could skip the water and treats. I quickly realized the pack, or the pug mafia as I so often referred to them, was not going to let me off the hook.

I learned never to break from routine with these guys. Contrary to all my readings about dogs, which say they have a toddler's intelligence level, they're a lot smarter than one might think. At least this group is, and one will cover for the other. "Hey man, this guy's forgetting about the treats. What are we gonna do about it?" I think the real reason behind this is in a quote I found on the internet about dogs: "To you, a dog is part of your life. To a dog, you are their entire life."

With everyone finally in bed and ready to settle down, there were only a few more things to do. I had to pet and scratch them all and tell them individually "good night," and I loved them. If I petted one more than another, I would get sulks, huffs, and wanting looks, so I had to do it equally.

Jaxon would always squirm his way between Diane and I so I could pet him first. Zoe is less demanding, requiring only an ear rub, while Rikah likes to be scratched all over. Max liked his ears scratched vigorously and was the only one to make "hmmmmm" noises while I did it. Then they would all find their spots. Zoe immediately claims the pillow next to me, which is a problem since she snores the loudest. The game for me is to try to get to sleep before she does, but I never make it. Sometimes, I have to reposition her so the business end is facing in another direction, but this isn't easy with a slumbering, twenty-six-pound dog. Jaxon will migrate to the foot of the bed with his girlfriend, Rikah. Lola likes to go under the covers, and the following morning, I have to search for her since she blends in so well. I had to clear a comfy spot next to me for Max, who'd do a few circles before plopping down with a thump. Sometimes he would wind up almost on top of me, but once Maxie was settled, he was good for the night. And he was a quiet, rhythmic sleeper.

Having everyone safe and snuggled in, with the varied pug noises hammering away, is a reassuring feeling for me. I have often been to Boothbay Harbor, Maine, and our snoring dogs remind me of the harbor's cadent foghorns on a misty night, each having their own pitch and timing.

These days, I think I miss Max the most at bedtime. When I see the other dogs sleeping soundly next to us, it's sad for me not to have Max there. I wish it were possible to have one more day with him, just to make sure he knew how much we loved and cared about him.

Just one more day.

Chapter 22

The Day the Angels Cried

"Max had so much more of his life left to live."

The unfortunate side of the silent contract one unwittingly signs when adopting pets is you agree to one day lose them. It's in the fine print, and it's required. "Just sign here." While I have tried to put this out of my mind while they are with us, as my pets get older, these thoughts gradually move to the fore. These have always been terrifying, paralyzing thoughts; something I try not to think about, but subconsciously, something I cannot avoid. Pets are family, and I think all of us who have had loving pets in our lives have difficulty dealing with this very real eventuality. It's the downside of having a big heart—it sometimes gets broken.

It was later in the day on a Sunday in September when I rushed Max to a twenty-four-hour hospital. He wasn't eating, he was very lethargic, and he wasn't walking or interacting with his usual vigor. In other words, he wasn't behaving like the happy Max I had come to know and love. His expression was almost like when I first met him: sad and worried. As I carried him to the car, all I could think of was, *Oh, no. Oh, no. Please, no.* While he was clearly sick, it seemed to me at the time, he was much too young to have acquired anything life-threatening. Max had so much more of his life left to live. I was worried, but I had high hopes. Everyone will rush to help and protect him, and we will get through this. Max, as he had before, will prevail once again. He had to. For himself, for us, for Rikah, and for the pack.

It was not to be.

Max spent the next six or so days in a well-reputed animal hospital, and as his time there became more protracted, my hopes began to wane. Max wasn't making his own blood, and he had undergone three blood transfusions during the week. None of the doctors could pinpoint with any accuracy what exactly the issue was, although it appeared Max's initial treatment as a puppy and his resulting chronic GI issues had caught up with him. As I spoke with several doctors over the phone, and they outlined potential courses of action, I tried not to tear up. It was clear doing anything invasive would have killed Max on the spot.

The other dogs sensed something was amiss. They knew, of course, one of their pack members was missing, but they also seemed to know I was upset, and as a group, they amassed to comfort me. Surprisingly, it was newbie Tucker who led the way. I loved them all even more for it.

But the worst part had nothing to do with me. All I could think about was Max's state of mind and what he was going through. Max hated doctors and hospitals. He would shake uncontrollably when he knew he was going to the vet, and he always knew. Dogs can sense that sort of thing. I knew Max well, and I didn't want him to feel the way he felt when we first met him—alone, frightened, abandoned, surrounded by uncertainty, and attended to by people he didn't know. And undoubtedly, he was also in pain and discomfort. I knew in my heart he would never recover from any illness under those circumstances. So, we would bring him familiar food. Diane asked the nurses to use phrases and nicknames Max recognized, and he seemed to respond to those with a smile. But still, the treatments weren't going anywhere, and later in the week, we were advised the third blood transfusion had little positive effect. Diane and I agreed if Max was not going to get any better at the hospital, then we should bring him back to familiar surroundings. I brought him home the following Saturday.

Max was in bad shape, although he was clearly happy to be home with us. I hoped he didn't think we had abandoned him just because he got sick. I think he was smart enough to realize that. He wasn't allowed to intermingle with the other dogs due to the toxicity of his medicine, so we set him up in the den. He was where he loved to be—Max's room in his forever home. He brightened up a bit, and his tongue was out, but he was still horribly sick. He wouldn't eat. He couldn't hold his water, and he could barely stand up. So, I would carry him outside to his familiar play space and sit with him. I tried not to let him see me cry, but he always knew when the people around him were sad. And I was heartbroken. I was losing him. I couldn't believe it.

I slept on the couch with Max that night since I didn't want him to have another horrific evening alone. I woke up at four o'clock in the morning that Sunday. As he had done so many times before during our relationship, Max had awakened me by merely his presence. He was facing me in the darkness with his head resting on my pillow. It was his typical loving gaze, but this time, I could see sadness and distance in his eyes as I tearfully scratched his ears. Max was saying goodbye.

As I sat with him later in the day on Sunday, I could see him begin to fade. He could no longer see, and he was struggling to breathe. I called Diane to come to the room quickly. I moved close to his ear and told him I loved him while petting his head. Minutes later, Maxie passed. My best friend was gone.

I buried him amongst our pine trees later that day, and just as I finished, it started to rain. It was a soft, somber rain, a perfect metaphor given my state of mind. I stood there, looking at the cold pile of dirt for a few minutes, almost not comprehending and not wanting to believe the reality of what had transpired during the preceding hours. It was one of the saddest moments in my life. I realized my small world would not be the same without him, and Max also hadn't even made his twelfth birthday. It was late September; it was getting dark earlier, and I had lost my companion, my best friend. As I stood alone under the canopy of our magnificent pines in the receding light of evening, the rain began to make its way to me.

Apparently, even the angels were crying.

Happier days

Chapter 23
A Tribute to Max

I know of no other who compares with you

It's been hard for me to get used to the reality that Max, the backward, clumsy, and frightened little puppy whose paws were too big, is gone. I often think back to that cold January night when we met and how he convinced me he needed me. I didn't realize at the time I needed him just as much. Had he not cast that loving gaze at me that first evening, our lives would have been quite different.

I will probably never lose this empty feeling of loss and sorrow. I will just have to learn to live with it and go on living without him, remembering the happy times we had. Max loved every minute of life, and it seems to me he deserved a longer one. Every day was a new adventure for Max, and I remember sometimes being jealous of his never-ending enthusiasm. Loving life is one of the great lessons I learned from Max, and seeing him love his so much over the years helped me love mine a little more. I resolved to be like him and to look forward to the excitement each new day may bring.

So far, it hasn't been easy.

The void left by Max's abrupt departure made us realize how central a figure he was in our house of crazy, lovable pets. Somehow, I didn't see it when he was with us, but I do now, and I'm still trying to figure out how he achieved this. Perhaps it was the excited way he welcomed everyone he met or how vigorously he pursued his daily ambitions. Or how easily he made everyone he came in contact with as happy as he was. Maybe it was his odd but amusing habits and inclinations that required an inordinate amount of our focus and attention.

No, the answer was right in front of me all along. And it should have been plainly obvious. As he did with me our very first night, Max's special gift lay in his amazing ability to communicate and in a language we could understand. He spoke to us each day for his entire life.

Ultimately, our world completely revolved around Max, almost as if he had intended it to be that way all along. The quintessential narcissist, he loved when things were "all about Max," and he and Rikah made sure they always were. I was always more than happy to oblige. There will never be another like him, and it is for this reason I feel privileged I somehow, against all odds, found him and was able to share some of my life with him. I am happy Diane and I were able to give him a chance at having a beautiful life. I think he had one.

When I arrive home these days, I sometimes expect to be greeted by his wagging tail and smile or see him come running in with the pack when I call them to dinner. When I take them all outside on a beautiful day, I am reminded of that amazing first spring with him and Rikah. As I watch our dogs run and play, I think of Max's free spirit, his love of the outdoors, his loving and gentle nature, and how he was able to forget those horrible first few months by finding happiness in his forever home with us.

I wake up every morning missing him. I go to bed each night missing him. And I miss him throughout each day. I am sure I will think of Max every day for the rest of my life. I will end my tribute by saying here what I said to him each night as we went to bed.

Good night, Max.

I love you, Max.

Chapter 24
On Rescuing a Dog

God sees you through a dog's eyes.

While I am not a particularly religious person, I do think the above saying is true.

Some of the stories of animal cruelty are so horrific, I cannot bear to read them. These are a sad statement on the human condition and on the view many take in respect to defenseless animals that cannot communicate, retaliate, or escape. My heart goes out to these creatures, especially now fully aware they have genuine feelings. Breeders and puppy mills seem to be the primary culprits and my first-hand experience with these corroborate this statement. Sure, there are some breeders who are ethical and considerate, but there are many others who are not.

And then there are the unofficial breeders who do it illegally for some quick cash to fund other illegal activities or habits. Still others raise dogs for fighting or use them as bait. These, in my opinion, are the most despicable. I have also read the stories of owners who abandon their faithful pets once they get old, and I don't understand how anyone could possibly do this. It makes my blood boil.

But I am, above all, a realist, and I know these things go on. All I can do is take in and love as many as I can, but it never seems like it's enough. While a society can make all the rules it wants to combat these abuses, the laws have to be enforced for them to work even a little. And then there's the fact you cannot legislate morality. How about leaving a pet with a shelter rather than abandoning it so at least the animal has something of a chance to survive?

The high cost of medicine and medical treatment has also acted to exacerbate the issue of abandonment, and offhand, there doesn't appear to be a good answer for this. I often reflect it is perhaps even more difficult to practice veterinary medicine than human medicine since the animals they are treating cannot tell a vet where it hurts. Only through careful analysis or perhaps through rather invasive procedures can a problem be identified with any accuracy. And the training, regulations, and cost to become a vet have become almost as extensive as they are for human health care providers. There are some, however, who provide such services at reduced fees out of the goodness of their hearts.

Making contributions to animal rescue organizations is somewhat of a mixed bag. While I have donated to some of the more prominent entities, I have found the smaller, local charities are more focused on the animals than they are on fancy marketing programs or as in the case of the ASPCA recently, flying around on corporate jets. Still, I find directly helping someone who has a pet is more rewarding, and the help has a better chance of getting to where it's needed.

So, while I am an advocate of people adopting pets in need, I implore them to make sure they first know and understand what it's all about beforehand. It can be expensive, and pets, dogs especially, can be needy, time consuming, and constraining. And I always recommend folks adopt rather than buying from a breeder. Please rescue a dog. Or a cat. Or maybe even a snake. There are so many creatures who need us.

Reflections on Writing

Writing is easy. All you have to do is cross out the wrong words.
—Mark Twain

While I have tried my best to relate the true essence and emotion of living with, caring for, and loving a bunch of crazy dogs, looking back upon all my reviewing, rewriting, and editing, it seems to me no amount of such could ever capture my experience effectively. Ignoring for a minute the fact I am in no way a professional writer, it became clear the words and photos contained in what is essentially an editorialized, factual account can only go so far. I remember thinking when I began writing soon after Max died, *How am I ever going to explain all this?*

In retrospect, perhaps I should have handed it all off to a creative writer who would be more capable than I of conveying the true human feeling of having a long-term relationship with beings that cannot speak. At least not English. But no, I just had to do this myself, whatever the outcome or result, for the simple fact this is, and I wanted it to be, my account and one that was firsthand. I feel an appropriate metaphor may be found in the difference between what one may experience in seeing a photo of the Alps versus actually seeing them in person. Photos or words, no matter how creatively or extensively presented, can simply not compare to the breathtaking experience of actually having been there. Such is the gap I have experienced throughout the writing of this book.

The other question constantly in play for me during this process was why would someone want to pick up this book and read it? The difference, I feel, is in one's ability to tell a story instead of merely presenting facts. A true story, methinks, is one having a meaningful confluence of multiple plots, humor, sadness, action, excitement, and surprise, all underpinned by an introspective insight into each of the players including, oftentimes, the writer. In short, a story that contains at least some of these varied elements makes one want to read more whereas a mere relation of factual data may not. Still, *The Story of Max* is mostly comprised of memoirs I tried to make more interesting by presenting the different perspectives of the players and by relating the triumphs and learning experiences had along the way.

Since my relationship with my dogs has been developed over a number of years, and I, therefore, knew them quite well, I found it difficult at times not to fall into the trap of assuming or inadvertently overlooking things about them. I tried instead, with perhaps varying levels of success, to step back from their antics and from my relationship with them as if I were a third-party observer, the proverbial "fly on the wall." This enabled me to critically recount and evaluate some of the more humorous, and sometimes not so humorous, aspects of both their personalities and inclinations as well as my own.

At other times, I attempted to see things as the dogs might have and then tried to convey my interpretation of their perception of the world to the reader. Writing from these perspectives helped me remember what I was thinking during a given situation. As a result, there were many "Oh, yeah, I remember that!" moments for me during the construct of this book and the memories of what I was feeling or experiencing at the time came flooding back. Once this began to happen, I could hardly write fast enough.

Certainly, I now understand the limitations that exist in any literary work. All I had were my words and some photos to convey the depth of my relationship with my dogs and establish a connection with them and the reader. Like my Alps example, I knew reading my story would never be the same as living it. Nevertheless, I hope readers are able to gain a glimpse of what it's like to love and live with these amazing creatures and how by doing so, we enhanced each other's lives.

My little trooper

Postscript

My Dear Little Lola

During the course of my writing and editing this book for publication, our sweet Lola passed away. She had made it past fifteen and died of natural causes, peacefully here with us in her presence one sad night in early November 2021. While I had initially felt our rescue home and care were merely a temporary refuge for her, we grew to love her as if she was one of our initial four.

And Lola certainly left her mark upon us. Despite the debilitating aspects of her advanced age, she was such a cheerful and determined creature. Rain, snow, long walks and our large, confusing single-story home had virtually no effect upon Lola's enthusiasm and her drive to occupy her place in the pack. I was so proud of her and happy Lola had finally found her nirvana.

I will miss her forever.

Nicknames

Rikah

Rikah Honey
Tas
Rik
The Boss
Super Dog

Max

Maxie
Maximus
Maxie Boy
The Big Dog
Bud
The Real Dog

Jaxon

Jax
Jaxie
Little Bud
Recon
Snaggle Tooth
Huckleberry
Mommy's Boy

Zoe

Zo-Zo
Zoe Girl
Zoe Dear
Zoe Bear
Zo-Zo Bear
Jo-Jo
Jo-Jo Bear
Zozie
Zoe Honey
Girlie

Zoe and Jaxon (collectively)

The Twins
My Beautiful Twins

Tucker

Tuck
Tucky
Tucker Bud
T- Bud
Bam-Bam
Rocket Dog
Bruiser

Lola

Lola Honey
Tiger
Hot Shot

The Pack (collectively)

The Pug Mafia

Author Bio

Robert J. Caso was born in Astoria Queens, New York. He attended Villanova and Lehigh Universities and has worked in finance for emerging growth companies for most of his professional life. He currently runs a consulting firm with his wife, Diane, and teaches Finance for Non-Finance Professionals.

For fun, Rob designs award-winning flying scale models and restores vintage cars and bikes. He loves to ride his motorcycles in the Alps, and he's also an avid aviation enthusiast. But by far, the most fulfilling experience he's ever had has been caring for his rescued pugs. He's been rescuing animals in need his entire life. By purchasing this book, you're contributing to that dream: 100 percent of the proceeds go directly to animal rescue efforts. Maybe you, too, will help someone's Max.

Made in the USA
Las Vegas, NV
26 April 2022

47972874R50066